CAREER
IDEAS
for kids who like
COMPUTERS

21680

MARANATHA CHRISTIAN ACADEMY

3800 S. FAIRVIEW RD.

SANTA ANA, CA 92704

(714) 556-0965

DEMCO

THE CAREER IDEAS FOR KIDS SERIES

Career Ideas for Kids Who Like Adventure and Travel, Second Edition
Career Ideas for Kids Who Like Animals and Nature, Second Edition
Career Ideas for Kids Who Like Art, Second Edition
Career Ideas for Kids Who Like Computers, Second Edition
Career Ideas for Kids Who Like Math and Money, Second Edition
Career Ideas for Kids Who Like Music and Dance, Second Edition
Career Ideas for Kids Who Like Science, Second Edition
Career Ideas for Kids Who Like Sports, Second Edition
Career Ideas for Kids Who Like Talking, Second Edition
Career Ideas for Kids Who Like Writing, Second Edition

Second Edition

DIANE LINDSEY REEVES
with
LINDSEY CLASEN

Illustrations by
NANCY BOND

Checkmark Books®
An imprint of Infobase Publishing

CAREER IDEAS FOR KIDS WHO LIKE COMPUTERS, Second Edition

Checkmark Books
An imprint of Infobase Publishing
132 West 31st Street
New York NY 10001

Library of Congress Cataloging-in-Publication Data

Reeves, Diane Lindsey, 1959–
  Career ideas for kids who like computers / Diane Lindsey Reeves with Lindsey Clasen; illustrations by Nancy Bond. — 2nd ed.
    p. cm — (The career ideas for kids series)
  Includes bibliographical references and index.
  ISBN-13: 978-0-8160-6543-1 (hc : alk. paper)
  ISBN-10: 0-8160-6543-8 (hc : alk. paper)
  ISBN-13: 978-0-8160-6544-8 (pb : alk. paper)
  ISBN-10: 0-8160-6544-6 (pb : alk. paper) 1. Computer science—Vocational guidance—Juvenile literature. I. Clasen, Lindsey. II. Bond, Nancy, ill. III. Title.
  QA76.25.R44 2007
  004.023—dc22   2007009719

Checkmark Books are available at special discounts when purchased in bulk quantities for businesses, associations, institutions, or sales promotions. Please call our Special Sales Department in New York at (212) 967-8800 or (800) 322-8755.

You can find Facts On File on the World Wide Web at http://www.factsonfile.com

Original text and cover design by Smart Graphics
Illustrations by Nancy Bond

Printed in the United States of America

MP Hermitage 10 9 8 7 6 5 4 3 2 1

This book is printed on acid-free paper.

CONTENTS

Acknowledgments   vii

Make a Choice!   1
    Choice A   2
    Choice B   2

How to Use This Book   3

Get in Gear!   7
    Discover #1: Watch for Signs Along the Way   7
    Discover #2: Rules of the Road   9
    Discover #3: Dangerous Detours   16
    Discover #4: Ultimate Career Destination   17
    Discover #5: Get Some Direction   18

Take a Trip!   27
    Artificial Intelligence Scientist   29
    Computer Game Designer   39
    Computer Programmer   48
    Hardware Engineer   56
    Internet Systems Administrator   64
    Multimedia Developer   73
    Online Researcher   81
    Repair Technician   88
    Software Entrepreneur   95
    Systems Analyst   104
    Systems Manager   112
    Technical Support Representative   119
    Technical Writer   128
    Trainer   136
    Webmaster   144

Make a Computer Detour!   153
     A World of Computer Careers   154

Don't Stop Now!   157
     #1 Narrow Down Your Choices   159
     #2 Surf the Net   159
     #3 Snoop at the Library   161
     #4 Get In Touch with the Experts   163
     #5 Chat on the Phone   165
     #6 Information is Power   169

What's Next?   173
     Rediscover #1: Watch for Signs Along the Way   174
     Rediscover #2: Rules of the Road   174
     Rediscover #3: Dangerous Detours   175
     Rediscover #4: Ultimate Career Destination   176
     Rediscover #5: Get Some Direction   176

Hooray! You Did It!   179

Some Future Destinations   181
     It's Not Just for Nerds   181
     Awesome Internet Career Resources   182
     Join the Club   185
     More Career Books Especially for Kids   185
     Heavy-Duty Resources   187
     Finding Places to Work   187

Index   189

A million thanks to the people who took the time to share their career stories and provide photos for this book:

Elias AbuGhazaleh
Brenda Dickson Curry
Rachel Drummond
Lowell Hawkinson
Amelia Kassel
Gary Kiliany
Rob Kolstad
Victor Kushdilian
Mike Little
John Pemberton
Molly Roberts
Art Roche
Jeni Li Shoecraft
Tim Vann
Will Wright

Finally, much appreciation and admiration is due to all the behind-the-scenes people at Ferguson who have done so much to make this series all that it is. With extra thanks to James Chambers and Sarah Fogarty.

MAKE A CHOICE!

Choices.

You make them every day. What do I want for breakfast? Which shirt can I pull out of the dirty-clothes hamper to wear to school today? Should I finish my homework or play video games?

Some choices don't make much difference in the overall scheme of things. Face it; who really cares whether you wear the blue shirt or the red one?

Other choices are a major big deal. Figuring out what you want to be when you grow up is one of those all-important choices.

But, you say, you're just a kid. How are you supposed to know what you want to do with your life?

You're right: 10, 11, 12, and even 13 are a bit young to know exactly what and where and how you're going to do whatever it is you're going to do as an adult. But it's the perfect time to start making some important discoveries about who you are, what you like to do, and what you do best. It's a great time to start exploring the options and experimenting with different ideas. In fact, there's never a better time to mess around with different career ideas without messing up your life.

When it comes to picking a career, you've basically got two choices.

CHOICE A

You can be like lots of other people and just go with the flow. Float through school doing only what you absolutely have to in order to graduate, take any job you can find, collect a pay-check, and meander your way to retirement without making much of a splash in life.

Although many people take this route and do just fine, others end up settling for second best. They miss out on a meaningful education, satisfying work, and the rewards of a focused and well-planned career. That's why this path is not an especially good idea for someone who actually wants to have a life.

CHOICE B

Other people get a little more involved in choosing a career. They figure out what they want to accomplish in their lives—whether it's making a difference, making lots of money, or simply enjoying what they do. Then they find out what it takes to reach that goal, and they set about doing it with gusto. It's kind of like these people do things on purpose instead of letting life happen by accident.

Choosing A is like going to an ice cream parlor where there are all kinds of awesome flavors and ordering a single scoop of plain vanilla. Going with Choice B is more like visiting that same ice cream parlor and ordering a super duper brownie sundae drizzled with hot fudge, smothered in whip cream, and topped with a big red cherry.

Do you see the difference?

Reading this book is a great idea for kids who want to go after life in a big way. It provides a first step toward learning about careers that match your skills, values, and dreams. It will help you make the most out of your time in school and maybe even inspire you to—as the U.S. Army so proudly says—"be all that you can be."

Ready for the challenge of Choice B? If so, read the next section for instructions on how to get started.

HOW TO USE THIS BOOK

This book isn't just about interesting careers that other people have. It's also a book about interesting careers that you can have.

Of course, it won't do you a bit of good to just read this book. To get the whole shebang, you're going to have to jump in with both feet, roll up your sleeves, put on your thinking cap—whatever it takes—to help you do these three things:

☼ Discover what you do best and enjoy the most. (This is the secret ingredient for finding work that's perfect for you.)

- ☼ Explore ways to match your interests and abilities with career ideas.
- ☼ Experiment with lots of different ideas until you find the ideal career. (It's like trying on all kinds of hats to see which ones fit!)

Use this book as a road map to some exciting career destinations. Here's what to expect in the chapters that follow.

GET IN GEAR!

First stop: discover. These activities will help you uncover important clues about the special traits and abilities that make you *you*. When you are finished you will have developed a personal Skill Set that will help guide you to career ideas in the next chapter.

TAKE A TRIP!

Next stop: explore. Cruise down the career idea highway and find out about a variety of career ideas that are especially appropriate for people who like computers. Use the Skill Set chart at the beginning of each career profile to match your own interests with those required for success on the job.

Once you've identified a career that interests you, kick your exploration into high gear by checking out some of the Web sites, library resources, and professional organizations listed at the end of each career profile. For an extra challenge, follow the instructions for the Try It Out activities.

MAKE A COMPUTER DETOUR!

Here's your chance to explore up-and-coming opportunities in computer science as well as the fields of system analysis, engineering, and other technical areas.

Just when you thought you'd seen it all, here come dozens of interesting art ideas to add to the career mix. Charge up

your career search by learning all you can about some of these opportunities.

DON'T STOP NOW!

Third stop: experiment. The library, the telephone, a computer, and a mentor—four keys to a successful career planning adventure. Use them well, and before long you'll be on the trail of some hot career ideas of your own.

WHAT'S NEXT?

Make a plan! Chart your course (or at least the next stop) with these career planning road maps. Whether you're moving full steam ahead with a great idea or get slowed down at a yellow light of indecision, these road maps will keep you moving forward toward a great future.

Use a pencil—you're bound to make a detour or two along the way. But, hey, you've got to start somewhere.

HOORAY! YOU DID IT!

Some final rules of the road before sending you off to new adventures.

SOME FUTURE DESTINATIONS

This section lists a few career planning tools you'll want to know about.

You've got a lot of ground to cover in this phase of your career planning journey. Start your engines and get ready for an exciting adventure!

Career planning is a lifelong journey. There's usually more than one way to get where you're going, and there are often some interesting detours along the way. But you have to start somewhere. So rev up and find out all you can about one-of-a-kind, specially designed you. That's the first stop on what can be the most exciting trip of your life!

To get started, complete the five exercises described throughout the following pages.

DISCOVER #1: WATCH FOR SIGNS ALONG THE WAY

Road signs help drivers figure out how to get where they want to go. They provide clues about direction, road conditions, and safety. Your career road signs will provide clues about who you are, what you like, and what you do best. These clues can help you decide where to look for the career ideas that are best for you.

Complete the following statements to make them true for you. There are no right or wrong reasons. Jot down the response that describes you best. Your answers will provide important clues about career paths you should explore.

Please Note: If this book does not belong to you, write your responses on a separate sheet of paper.

On my last report card, I got the best grade in _____ .

On my last report card, I got the worst grade in _____ .

I am happiest when _____ .

Something I can do for hours without getting bored is _____ .

Something that bores me out of my mind is
_____ .

My favorite class is _____ .

My least favorite class is_____ .

The one thing I'd like to accomplish is
_____ .

My favorite thing to do after school is
_____ .

My least favorite thing to do after school
is _____ .

Something I'm really good at is _____ .

Something really tough for me to do
is _____ .

My favorite adult person is _____
because _____ .

When I grow up _____ .

The kinds of books I like to read are
about _____ .

The kinds of videos I like to watch are
about _____ .

DISCOVER #2: RULES OF THE ROAD

Pretty much any job you can think of involves six common ingredients. Whether the work requires saving the world or selling bananas, all work revolves around a central **purpose** or reason for existing. All work is conducted somewhere, in some **place**, whether it's on the 28th floor of a city sky-scraper or on a cruise ship in the middle of an ocean. All work requires a certain **time** commitment and is performed using various types of **tools**. **People** also play an important part in most jobs—whether the job involves interacting with lots or very few of them. And, especially from where you are sitting as a kid still in school, all work involves some type of **preparation** to learn how to do the job.

Another word for these six common ingredients is "values." Each one represents important aspects of work that people value in different ways. The following activity will give you a chance to think about what matters most to you in each of these areas. That way you'll get a better idea of things to look for as you explore different careers.

Here's how the process works:

First, read the statements listed for each value on the following pages. Decide which, if any, represent your idea of an ideal job.

Next, take a look at the grid on page 16. For every value statement with which you agreed, draw its symbol in the appropriate space on your grid. (If this book doesn't belong to you, use a blank sheet of paper to draw your own grid with six big spaces.) Or, if you want to get really fancy, cut pictures out of magazines and glue them into the appropriate space. If you do not see a symbol that represents your best answer, make up a new one and sketch it in the appropriate box.

When you are finished, you'll have a very useful picture of the kinds of values that matter most to you in your future job.

PURPOSE		
Which of the following statements describes what you most hope to accomplish in your future work? Pick as many as are true for you and feel free to add others.		
♥	❏	I want to help other people.
💵	❏	I want to make lots of money.
★	❏	I want to do something I really believe in.
✋	❏	I want to make things.
🧠	❏	I want to use my brain power in challenging ways.
💡	❏	I want to work with my own creative ideas.
🏆	❏	I want to be very successful.
🛝	❏	I want to find a good company and stick with it for the rest of my life.
🔦	❏	I want to be famous.
Other purpose-related things that are especially important to me are		

PLACE

When you think about your future work, what kind of place would you most like to do it in? Pick as many as are true for you and feel free to add others.

⛬	☐	I want to work in a big city skyscraper.
	☐	I want to work in a shopping mall or retail store.
	☐	I want to work in the great outdoors.
	☐	I want to travel a lot for my work.
	☐	I want to work out of my own home.
	☐	I want to work for a govern-ment agency.
	☐	I want to work in a school or university.
	☐	I want to work in a factory or laboratory.

Other place-related things that are especially important to me are

TIME

When you think about your future work, what kind of schedule sounds most appealing to you? Pick as many as are true for you and feel free to add others.

	❑	I'd rather work regular business hours—nine to five, Monday through Friday.
	❑	I'd like to have lots of vacation time.
	❑	I'd prefer a flexible schedule so I can balance my work, family, and personal needs.
	❑	I'd like to work nights only so my days are free.
	❑	I'd like to work where the pace is fast and I stay busy all day.
	❑	I'd like to work where I would always know exactly what I'm supposed to do.
	❑	I'd like to work where I could plan my own day.
	❑	I'd like to work where there's lots of variety and no two days are alike.

Other time-related things that are especially important to me are

TOOLS

What kinds of things would you most like to work with? Pick as many as are true for you and feel free to add others.

🧍	❑	I'd prefer to work mostly with people.
🖥	❑	I'd prefer to work mostly with technology.
🔩	❑	I'd prefer to work mostly with machines.
🛍	❑	I'd prefer to work mostly with products people buy.
✈	❑	I'd prefer to work mostly with planes, trains, automobiles, or other things that go.
🗣	❑	I'd prefer to work mostly with ideas.
📖	❑	I'd prefer to work mostly with information.
🌳	❑	I'd prefer to work mostly with nature.

Other tool-related things that are especially important to me are

	❏	I'd like to work with lots of people all day long.
	❏	I'd prefer to work alone most of the time.
	❏	I'd like to work as part of a team.
	❏	I'd like to work with people I might choose as friends.
	❏	I'd like to work with babies, children, or teenagers,
	❏	I'd like to work mostly with elderly people.
	❏	I'd like to work mostly with people who are in trouble.
	❏	I'd like to work mostly with people who are ill.

PEOPLE

What role do other people play in your future work? How many do you want to interact with on a daily basis? What age group would you most enjoy working with? Pick as many as are true for you and feel free to add others.

Other people-related things that are especially important to me are

PREPARATION

When you think about your future work, how much time and energy do you want to devote to preparing for it? Pick as many as are true for you and feel free to add others.

🎓	❏	I want to find a job that requires a college degree.
🤝	❏	I want to find a job where I could learn what I need to know on the job.
🎗	❏	I want to find a job that requires no additional training after I graduate from high school.
🪜	❏	I want to find a job where the more education I get, the better my chances for a better job.
BOSS	❏	I want to run my own business and be my own boss.

Other preparation-related things that are especially important to me are

Now that you've uncovered some word clues about the types of values that are most important to you, use the grid on the following page (or use a separate sheet of paper if this book does not belong to you) to "paint a picture" of your ideal future career. Use the icons as ideas for how to visualize each statement. Or, if you'd like to get really creative, get a large sheet of paper, some markers, magazines, and glue or tape and create a collage.

PURPOSE	PLACE	TIME

TOOLS	PEOPLE	PREPARATION

DISCOVER #3: DANGEROUS DETOURS

Half of figuring out what you do want to do is figuring out what you don't want to do. Get a jump start on this process by making a list of 10 careers you already know you absolutely don't want to do.

Warning: Failure to heed early warnings signs to avoid careers like this can result in long hours of boredom and frustration spent doing a job you just weren't meant to do.

(If this book does not belong to you, make your list on a separate sheet of paper.)

1. _____ _____

2. _____ _____

3. _____ _____

4. _____   _____

5. _____   _____

6. _____   _____

7. _____   _____

8. _____   _____

9. _____   _____

10. _____   _____

Red Flag Summary:
Look over your list, and in second column above (or on a separate sheet of paper) see if you can summarize what it is about these jobs that makes you want to avoid them like a bad case of cooties.

DISCOVER #4: ULTIMATE CAREER DESTINATION

Imagine that your dream job is like a favorite tourist destination and you have to convince other people to pick it over every other career in the world. How would you describe it? What features make it especially appealing to you? What does a person have to do to have a career like it?

Take a blank sheet of paper and fold it into thirds. Fill each column on both sides with words and pictures that create a vivid image of what you'd most like your future career to be.

Special note: Just for now, instead of actually naming a specific career, describe what your ideal career would be like. In places where the name of the career would be used, leave a blank space like this _____. For instance: For people who want to become rich and famous, being a _____ is the way to go.

DISCOVER #5: GET SOME DIRECTION

It's easy to get lost when you don't have a good idea of where you want to go. This is especially true when you start thinking about what to do with the rest of your life. Unless you focus on where you want to go, you might get lost or even miss the exit. This discover exercise will help you connect your own interests and abilities with a whole world of career opportunities.

Mark the activities that you enjoy doing or would enjoy doing if you had the chance. Be picky. Don't mark ideas that you wish you would do. Mark only those that you would really do. For instance, if skydiving sounds appealing but you'd never do it because you are terrified of heights, don't mark it.

Please Note: If this book does not belong to you, write your responses on a separate sheet of paper.

- ❏ 1. Rescue a cat stuck in a tree
- ❏ 2. Visit the pet store every time you go to the mall
- ❏ 3. Paint a mural on the cafeteria wall
- ❏ 4. Run for student council
- ❏ 5. Send e-mail to a "pen pal" in another state
- ❏ 6. Survey your classmates to find out what they do after school
- ❏ 7. Try out for the school play
- ❏ 8. Dissect a frog and identify the different organs
- ❏ 9. Play baseball, soccer, football, or _____ (fill in your favorite sport)

18

❏ 10. Talk on the phone to just about anyone who will talk back

❏ 11. Try foods from all over the world—Thailand, Poland, Japan, etc.

❏ 12. Write poems about things happening in your life

❏ 13. Create a really scary haunted house to take your friends through on Halloween

❏ 14. Recycle all your family's trash

❏ 15. Bake a cake and decorate it for your best friend's birthday

❏ 16. Sell enough advertisements for the school year-book to win a trip to Walt Disney World

❏ 17. Simulate an imaginary flight through space on your computer screen

❏ 18. Build model airplanes, boats, doll houses, or anything from kits

❏ 19. Teach your friends a new dance routine

❏ 20. Watch the stars come out at night and see how many constellations you can find

❏ 21. Watch baseball, soccer, football, or _____ (fill in your favorite sport) on TV

❏ 22. Give a speech in front of the entire school

❏ 23. Plan the class field trip to Washington, D.C.

❏ 24. Read everything in sight, including the back of the cereal box

❏ 25. Figure out "who dunnit" in a mystery story

❏ 26. Take in stray or hurt animals

❏ 27. Make a poster announcing the school football game

❏ 28. Think up a new way to make the lunch line move faster and explain it to the cafeteria staff

❏ 29. Put together a multimedia show for a school assembly using music and lots of pictures and graphics

❏ 30. Invest your allowance in the stock market and keep track of how it does

❏ 31. Go to the ballet or opera every time you get the chance

❏ 32. Do experiments with a chemistry set

❏ 33. Keep score at your sister's Little League game

❏ 34. Use lots of funny voices when reading stories to children

❑ 35. Ride airplanes, trains, boats—anything that moves

❑ 36. Interview the new exchange student for an article in the school newspaper

❑ 37. Build your own treehouse

❑ 38. Help clean up a waste site in your neighborhood

❑ 39. Visit an art museum and pick out your favorite painting

❑ 40. Play Monopoly in an all-night championship challenge

❑ 41. Make a chart on the computer to show how much soda students buy from the school vending machines each week

❑ 42. Keep track of how much your team earns to buy new uniforms

❑ 43. Play an instrument in the school band or orchestra

❑ 44. Take things apart and put them back together again

❑ 45. Write stories about sports for the school newspaper

❑ 46. Listen to other people talk about their problems

❑ 47. Imagine yourself in exotic places

❑ 48. Hang around bookstores and libraries

❏ 49. Play harmless practical jokes on April Fools' Day
❏ 50. Join the 4-H club at your school
❏ 51. Take photographs at the school talent show
❏ 52. Make money by setting up your own business—paper route, lemonade stand, etc.
❏ 53. Create an imaginary city using a computer
❏ 54. Do 3-D puzzles
❏ 55. Keep track of the top 10 songs of the week
❏ 56. Read about famous inventors and their inventions
❏ 57. Make play-by-play announcements at the school football game
❏ 58. Answer phones during a telethon to raise money for orphans
❏ 59. Be an exchange student in another country
❏ 60. Write down all your secret thoughts and favorite sayings in a journal
❏ 61. Jump out of an airplane (with a parachute, of course)
❏ 62. Plant and grow a garden in your backyard (or windowsill)
❏ 63. Use a video camera to make your own movies

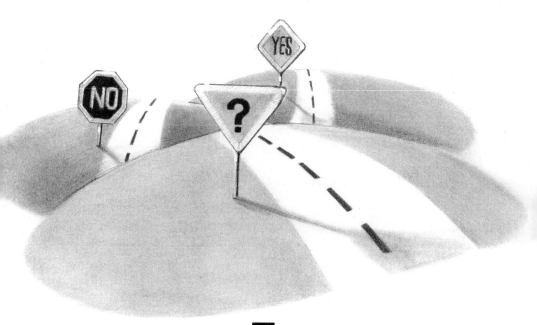

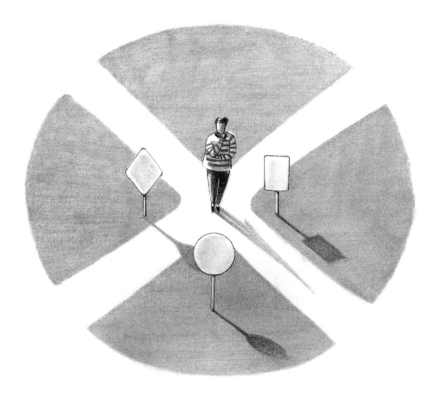

❏ 64. Get your friends together to help clean up your town after a hurricane or other natural disaster

❏ 65. Spend your summer at a computer camp learning lots of new computer programs

❏ 66. Build bridges, skyscrapers, and other structures out of LEGOs

❏ 67. Plan a concert in the park for little kids

❏ 68. Collect different kinds of rocks

❏ 69. Help plan a sports tournament

❏ 70. Be DJ for the school dance

❏ 71. Learn how to fly a plane or sail a boat

❏ 72. Write funny captions for pictures in the school yearbook

❏ 73. Scuba dive to search for buried treasure

❏ 74. Recognize and name several different breeds of cats, dogs, and other animals

❏ 75. Sketch pictures of your friends

❑ 76. Pick out neat stuff to sell at the school store
❑ 77. Answer your classmates' questions about how to use the computer
❑ 78. Draw a map showing how to get to your house from school
❑ 79. Make up new words to your favorite songs
❑ 80. Take a hike and name the different kinds of trees, birds, or flowers
❑ 81. Referee intramural basketball games
❑ 82. Join the school debate team
❑ 83. Make a poster with postcards from all the places you went on your summer vacation
❑ 84. Write down stories that your grandparents tell you about when they were young

CALCULATE THE CLUES

Now is your chance to add it all up. Each of the 12 boxes on the following pages contains an interest area that is common to both your world and the world of work. Follow these directions to discover your personal Skill Set:

1. Find all of the numbers that you checked on pages 18–23 in the following boxes and mark

them with an X. Work your way all the way through number 84.

2. Go back and count the Xs marked for each interest area. Write that number in the space that says "Total."
3. Find the interest area with the highest total and put a number one in the "Rank" blank of that box. Repeat this process for the next two highest scoring areas. Rank the second highest as number two and the third highest as number three.
4. If you have more than three strong areas, choose the three that are most important and interesting to you.

Remember: If this book does not belong to you, write your responses on a separate sheet of paper.

ADVENTURE	ANIMALS & NATURE	ART
❏ 1	❏ 2	❏ 3
❏ 13	❏ 14	❏ 15
❏ 25	❏ 26	❏ 27
❏ 37	❏ 38	❏ 39
❏ 49	❏ 50	❏ 51
❏ 61	❏ 62	❏ 63
❏ 73	❏ 74	❏ 75
Total: _____	Total: _____	Total: _____
Rank: _____	Rank: _____	Rank: _____

BUSINESS

❏ 4
❏ 16
❏ 28
❏ 40
❏ 52
❏ 64
❏ 76
Total: _____
Rank: _____

COMPUTERS

❏ 5
❏ 17
❏ 29
❏ 41
❏ 53
❏ 65
❏ 77
Total: _____
Rank: _____

MATH

❏ 6
❏ 18
❏ 30
❏ 42
❏ 54
❏ 66
❏ 78
Total: _____
Rank: _____

MUSIC/DANCE

❏ 7
❏ 19
❏ 31
❏ 43
❏ 55
❏ 67
❏ 79
Total: _____
Rank: _____

SCIENCE

❏ 8
❏ 20
❏ 32
❏ 44
❏ 56
❏ 68
❏ 80
Total: _____
Rank: _____

SPORTS

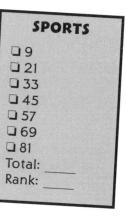

❏ 9
❏ 21
❏ 33
❏ 45
❏ 57
❏ 69
❏ 81
Total: _____
Rank: _____

TALKING

❏ 10
❏ 22
❏ 34
❏ 46
❏ 58
❏ 70
❏ 82
Total: _____
Rank: _____

TRAVEL

❏ 11
❏ 23
❏ 35
❏ 47
❏ 59
❏ 71
❏ 83
Total: _____
Rank: _____

WRITING

❏ 12
❏ 24
❏ 36
❏ 48
❏ 60
❏ 72
❏ 84
Total: _____
Rank: _____

What are your top three interest areas? List them here (or on a separate piece of paper).

    1. _____

    2. _____

    3. _____

This is your personal Skill Set and provides important clues about the kinds of work you're most likely to enjoy. Remember it and look for career ideas with a skill set that matches yours most closely. You'll find a Skill Set box at the beginning of each career profile in the following section.

TAKE A TRIP!

Quick! How many jobs can you think of that don't use computers? Chances are your list will be pretty short because computers have completely revolutionized the workplace. Almost every business, from gas stations and restaurants to airlines and government agencies, uses computers to perform very important on-the-job functions.

This section profiles some of the major career options in computers today; however, this list is just the beginning. And chances are that the career you'll have in computers in the next several years doesn't even exist right now. That's how fast the technology industry changes.

Use these ideas as a first step to discovering the computer career that's right for you.

As you read about each career, imagine yourself doing the job, and ask yourself the following questions:

- ☼ Would I like it?
- ☼ Would I be good at it?
- ☼ Is it the stuff my career dreams are made of?

If so, make a quick exit to explore what it involves, try it out, check it out, and get acquainted! Look out for the symbols below.

Buckle up and enjoy the trip!

 TRY IT OUT

 CHECK IT OUT

 ON THE WEB

 AT THE LIBRARY

 WITH THE EXPERTS

A NOTE ON WEB SITES
Internet sites tend to move around the Web a bit. If you have trouble finding a particular site, use an Internet browser to find a specific Web site or type of information.

Artificial Intelligence Scientist

WHAT IS AN ARTIFICIAL INTELLIGENCE SCIENTIST?

First things first. Before you can consider a career in artificial intelligence, you'll need to understand what artificial intelligence, or AI, is. In a nutshell, AI is the application of computer science and other sciences to make machines imitate what people do by programming intelligent behavior.

That means that artificial intelligence scientists are, in effect, teachers. The difference between them and your teachers at school is that their students are computers instead of people. Their job is to teach computers to think like very smart humans.

Artificial intelligence has been around for a while—it began in the late 1950s. But until recently the only way to work in this exciting field was to be involved in research, because AI promised more than it could deliver for a long time. These days AI is at work in many walks of life—from medicine to the food industry—and the field is growing fast. For instance, AI systems are used by Nabisco to bake their chocolate chip cookies. A computer has been programmed to examine every aspect of the process: It checks how much of each ingredient is going into each batch, whether the temperature is just right for baking consistently crisp cookies, and so forth. When something in the process gets out of kilter, the computer has to figure out how to fix it—pronto.

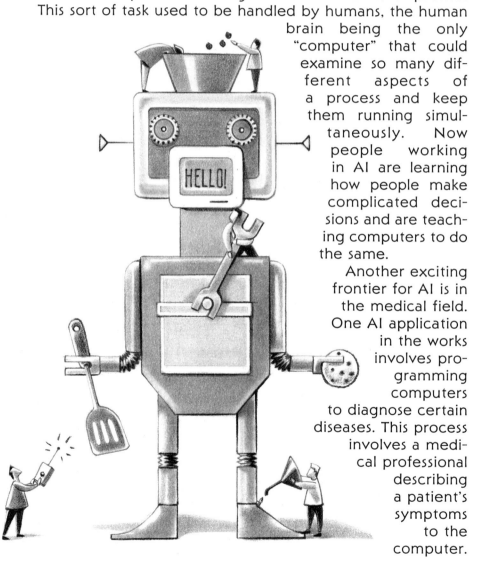

This sort of task used to be handled by humans, the human brain being the only "computer" that could examine so many different aspects of a process and keep them running simultaneously. Now people working in AI are learning how people make complicated decisions and are teaching computers to do the same.

Another exciting frontier for AI is in the medical field. One AI application in the works involves programming computers to diagnose certain diseases. This process involves a medical professional describing a patient's symptoms to the computer.

The computer asks questions based on the original information, considers the possibilities, provides a diagnosis, and prescribes a course of medicine or treatment. Obviously, technology like this could have a major impact on health care programs all over the world. Today AI affects everything from the war on terrorism and national security to cell phones and home appliances.

AI projects like these and others start with some very detailed analysis of the problem and proposed solutions. This process is called "modeling" and involves creating a computer model of the entire process. Models are complex mathematical equations that define how a process works (for example, how cookies get baked or how the body reacts to infectious disease). The model isn't complete until it is as close to reality as possible. Once an accurate model has been created, AI scientists must "teach" the computer how to react to changes in a useful manner.

If you enjoy playing computer games, you may already be using AI programs without realizing it. *SimCity* and *SimEarth* are great examples of relatively simple AI programs. These games are models—of the earth or a fictional city. They're not perfect, of course (planets and cities are incredibly complex systems), but they are "working" models. Add energy to the planet, and you'll get some kind of reaction; create an earthquake in the city, and you'll get another. Add your input, and the computer game directs the development of the planet accordingly.

You may have guessed by now that artificial intelligence is an especially demanding computer field. The work involves very complex thinking and the most sophisticated computer skills—there isn't much room for novices here. AI scientists have to know their stuff, starting with the most basic programming courses that are often offered at the high school level and moving toward "object-oriented" languages such as Java. Eventually, AI scientists must learn how complex computer systems function and must work with lots of advanced software programs, such as voice recognition, computer vision, language translation programs, and so on. Anything that humans do is fair game for an AI application. Now, if someone could just program a computer to do homework. . . .

 **TRY IT OUT**

COMPUTERIZED COOKIES

If Nabisco can use computers to bake chocolate chip cookies, so can you!

First, find a recipe for chocolate chip cookies. If your family doesn't have a favorite, just look on the back of a bag of chocolate chips. Read the recipe carefully. Or go online to http://www.webterrace.com/cookie/recipes.htm to find a variety of chocolate chip cookie recipes.

Now go back and think of all the different ways people might interpret the instructions. Add all the mistakes people might make, for instance, adding too much sugar or not enough butter. Maybe they get called to the phone and leave the cookies in the oven too long, or the stove isn't adjusted correctly and the temperature is lower than it should be. Perhaps they live in Denver, a mile above sea level, where baking works differently than it does elsewhere. Perhaps the chef didn't close the oven door completely after checking on the cookies. As you can see, there are quite a few ways to change the process.

Think of as many possibilities as you can and list them on one-half of a sheet of paper. On the other half, write instructions that can get the process "back on track." Putting the cookies back in for so many minutes, adjusting the temperature, and adding a particular quantity of another ingredient are a few possible solutions.

Finish the process and you will have completed a process similar to the one AI scientists use when modeling ways for computers to "think" through specific tasks.

✔ CHECK IT OUT

🖱 ON THE WEB

SMART WEB SITES

Artificial intelligence is everywhere and it's here to stay. Find out more about it at some of these kid-friendly Web sites:

- 💡 http://www.kids.net.au/encyclodedia-wiki/ai/Artificial_Intelligence
- 💡 http://www.thetech.org/exhibits_events/online/robots/teaser
- 💡 http://spaceplace.jpl.nasa.gov/en/kids/muses2.shtml
- 💡 http://prime.jsc.nasa.gov/ROV
- 💡 http://www.occdsb.on.ca/proj4632/kids.htm

COMPUTER CHAT

An AI chatbot or chatterbot is an online "robot" that uses artificial intelligence to imitate human conversation in a natural and enjoyable way. See what all the chat is about at some of these chatterbot Web sites.

- 💡 Communicate with a new computer pal at http://www.Jabberwacky.com.
- 💡 Have a chat with Alice, an online robot at http://alicebot.org.
- 💡 Meet Alan, the chatterbox, at http://www.a-i.com/alan.
- 💡 And, finally, find out what William Shakespeare has to say at http://www.shakespearebot.com.

YOU'VE GOT QUESTIONS, THEY'VE GOT ANSWERS

Get acquainted with some smart computers at Web sites that use artificial intelligence to provide answers to a wide (and sometimes wild!) variety of questions posed by curious Web surfers like you. A few to explore:

- 💡 Twenty Questions at http://www.20q.net.
- 💡 Brain boost at http://www.brainboost.com.

- Start, the world's first Web-based question answering system, has been going strong since 1993 and can be found at http://start.csail.mit.edu.
- When all else fails, go to Ask.com at http://www.ask.com.

LEARN AN AI PROGRAMMING LANGUAGE

There's actually an AI language designed for children of all ages: it's called Logo. This programming language is similar to LISP, the original AI language. You can download evaluation copies of Logo for free, for both PCs and Macs. To find out how, go to http://www.softronix.com/logo.html or http://www.magicsquare.com/LM2/try.htm.

Other interesting kid-friendly programming products that offer free demos include:

- Stagecast, where you can create your own video games and simulations at http://www.stagecast.com
- AgentSheets, where you can build interactive simulations for the Web: http://www.agentsheets.com
- Game Factory, where you design easy and fun software at http://www.clickteam.com/English/tgf.htm

 AT THE LIBRARY

AI BASICS

Build your knowledge about artificial intelligence by reading books such as:

Allman, Toney. *From Bug Legs to Walking Robots: Imitating Nature.* Farmington Hills, Mich.: Kid Haven, 2005.
Bridgman, Roger. *Robots.* New York: DK Publishing, 2005.
Brown, Jordan. *Robo World: The Story of Robot Designer Cynthia Breazeal.* Danbury, Conn.: Franklin Watts, 2005.
Clive, Gifford. *How to Build a Robot.* Danbury, Conn.: Franklin Watts, 2001.

Jeffries, David. *Artificial Intelligence: Robotics and Machine Evolution*. New York: Crabtree Publishing, 1999.
Margulies, Phillip. *Artificial Intelligence: Science on the Edge*. Woodbridge, Conn.: Blackbirch Press, 2003.
Perry, Robert L. *Artificial Intelligence*. Danbury, Conn.: Franklin Watts, 2000.
Wolf, Alex: *Artificial Intelligence: The Impact on Our Lives*. Chicago: Raintree, 2003.

ROBOTIC READS

Let your imagination run wild with some of the fictional characters featured in books such as:

Figueroa, Acton, and Phil Mendez. *Robots: Meet the Robots*. New York: Harper Entertainment, 2005.
Kirk, David. *Cosmic Play Dates*. New York: Grossett and Dunlap, 2005.
Munzer, Steve. *Robotz*. New York: Chicken House, 2002.
Schwarz, Haller. *Biode: No Kid on Earth Ever Brought His Computer to Life Until Justin*. Long Beach, Calif.: Prototype Entertainment Products, 2004.
Horumarin. *Boy and His Bot: Medabots*. San Francisco, Calif.: VIZ Media, 2002.

WITH THE EXPERTS

American Association for Artificial Intelligence
445 Burgess Drive
Menlo Park, CA 94025-3442
http://www.aaai.org

IEEE Systems, Man, and Cybernetics Society
445 Hoes Lane
Piscataway, NJ 08854-1331
http://www.ieee.org

GET ACQUAINTED

Lowell Hawkinson, Artificial
Intelligence Scientist

CAREER PATH

CHILDHOOD ASPIRATION:
To be a scientist who makes
an important contribution to
scientific knowledge.

FIRST JOB: Leader on a
research and development
project to develop the LISP 2
programming language.

CURRENT JOB: Chairman and
CTO (Chief Technology Officer) of Gensym Corp.

AN EARLY START

Lowell Hawkinson's involvement in AI goes back a long way,
almost to the beginning of the technology. AI research began
in the late 1950s at the Massachusetts Institute of Technology (MIT); Hawkinson appeared on the research scene while
studying physics at Yale in 1962. He had met someone who
was working with the early AI pioneers and became so fascinated with the subject that he decided to build his own
version of LISP, the original AI programming language. In
fact, LISP AI began to take up most of his time as the excitement of this new world displaced his interest in his original
studies.

Hawkinson's first job in AI was developing LISP for the U.S.
Department of Defense, under the auspices of the Advanced
Research Projects Agency (ARPA), the same group that set up
the Internet. Then, after several years of involvement in various software development projects, he became a research
associate at MIT's Laboratory for Computer Science, working

on natural language and natural language processing, two important areas of AI research.

INTO THE REAL WORLD

Since then he's spent more than two decades working in the artificial intelligence industry, bringing AI out of the universities and into cookie factories, automobile plants, and the Internet. For a while Hawkinson worked for LISP Machines Inc., an AI company founded by researchers from MIT. Then in 1986, he and several other people from LISP Machines founded Gensym, the company that Hawkinson heads today. This company calls itself "a leading supplier of software and services for intelligent systems that help organizations manage and optimize complex dynamic processes." That may sound complicated, but it could also be described as "we help DuPont make fibers, Motorola manage communication satellites, and Nabisco bake cookies."

THE FUTURE OF COMPUTING

Hawkinson believes that AI is the future of computing: "This is where computers are going. There's a lot of work to be done in the 21st century to make ordinary systems more and more intelligent." AI will play an essential role in making computers understand our voices, for instance, or recognize what they see through video cameras. Not only has AI got an exciting future, but it's already had a big impact on the computer business. "AI has been a spawning ground for many advanced technologies," he says. "Graphical window systems, for instance, came from within the context of AI research projects."

The Internet is an example of a problem waiting for an AI solution." "Everyone understands that information coming through the Internet, for example, will be pervasive," he remarks. "We're going to see incredible amounts of information available as raw data. What will set apart successful organizations will be the intelligent use of the data. Artificial intelligence is going to help us deal with what's been called 'info-glut.'" AI will be used to create more intelligent devices, machines that will help us handle far more information than we could ever hope to deal with by ourselves.

In addition, Hawkinson says we can expect to see AI incorporated into more and more everyday products. He says common household items will get smarter through AI and that there is plenty of opportunity awaiting future AI scientists with an interest in computers, electronics, and intelligence.

Computer Game Designer

SHORTCUTS

GO to http://www.yahooligans.com and search for "computer game." Be prepared to spend hours exploring all the fun links you'll find!

READ about how Nintendo Revolution (a video game console) works at http://entertainment.howstuffworks.com/nintendo_revolution.htm.

TRY making up new rules for a favorite game and notice how it changes things.

WHAT IS A COMPUTER GAME DESIGNER?

You mean, some people get paid to create computer games? Yep! Computer game designers enjoy the dream job of many a kid who loves computers. Creating computer games can be very challenging and a whole lot of fun.

In the early days of computer games, a single person could create a game. These days, teams are used to create them. In some cases, huge teams—similar to the sorts of teams that make movies—are required to put together sophisticated computer games. In fact, high-budget computer games cost more to create than low-budget movies. (Wing Commander reportedly cost 17 million dollars to make!)

The computer game designer develops and, in many cases, programs the game. The designer is often working alongside artists, writers, programmers, music and sound design staff, and even actors in some cases. Designing a computer game can be fascinating work; there's much more to it than meets the eye. It begins with the basic idea behind the game. Then there's the object of the game—what the player must do to win—and the obstacles of the game—what the computer does

to keep the player from winning. The graphics and sound effects are also a big part of the entire creative package. In short, a lot of work must happen before the play begins!

There are basic requirements for a career in computer games: a creative imagination and a background in computer programming. Don't let the second requirement scare you off. Programming doesn't have to be complicated. Think of it as playing with building blocks. You learn a number of simple commands first. Then you combine and link the commands to build something—one block at a time.

One way to test your aptitude for computer programming is to learn how to use a programming language called Logo. This language is designed as a first experience for kids but is sophisticated enough to use for years. If you decide that computer games are in your future, you'll eventually want to learn more "mainstream" programming languages, such as Visual Basic, C, or C++.

Learning about computer graphics and file formats can be helpful too. Computer games are similar to multimedia in that they require the use of a large number of different programs, media types, and file formats, which often leads to problems. The more familiar you are with multimedia, the more easily you'll be able to deal with the problems when they arise.

One more thing: Math can be very helpful too. Math is used to create algorithms, step-by-step problem-solving procedures that are essential to game programming. So as you pay a little more attention in math class, just think of it as learning the skills you'll use in your computer game career.

 **TRY IT OUT**

ONCE UPON A GAME

An essential first step that computer game designers use to develop ideas for new games is called storyboarding. This process involves using words and pictures to "tell the story" of the game and includes details about characters, the way the game is played, and other essential elements. See if you can come up with an idea for a computer game you'd love to play. Use index cards or sticky-notes to write down the sequence of action from the time a player sits down in front of their computer to the time they either win or lose the game.

LEARN THE LINGO

Logo, the kid's programming language, provides a very quick way to get involved in programming. It allows you to begin controlling the actions of people and animals within a few minutes of beginning work. You don't need to study the language for months before you can do anything; you can get started almost immediately.

A number of versions of Logo are available, some of which are free. Your school may already have Logo, or you can download it from the Internet. Try these sites to get a copy of Logo.

☀ Logo for Kids at http://www.snee.com/logo/logo4kids. pdf

- Magic Square at http://www.magicsquare.com/LM2/try.htm
- Softronix at http://www.softronix.com/logo.html

✔ CHECK IT OUT

🖱 ON THE WEB

START A COMPUTER GAME CLUB

Start a computer game club with a few friends. What for? To create a club library so that members can borrow new games. Everyone shares his or her computer games because it's fun and perfectly legal, as long as the game is only being used on one computer at a time. Make sure to set rules and insist that everyone abide by them to avoid problems. This way, everyone gets to play with the latest and greatest games without having to buy all of them.

At your club meetings, talk about the various games and find out what the other kids think about them. Put your heads together and try to figure out how each game works. Then think up ways to improve the games.

Once the group has existed for a while and has a regular membership, try writing to the game companies and asking for demo software. Your club's expertise can help them work the kinks out of a particular game and figure out the best way to reach their audience—other kids just like you.

Contests are another exciting way to keep the club going. Encourage members to learn Logo and use it to create simple games for each other to try out. Great practice and great fun. What are you waiting for?

To try out some free online games especially for kids go to:

- http://www.kidsdomain.com/games
- http://www.valuworld.com/kidsclub4kids/computergames.htm

☼ http://www.aplusmath.com/games
☼ http://www.agameaday.com/kidshome.html

And join the club at http://www.gzkidzone.com/register/
kidregister.asp.

BEST GAME ONLINE

For a sneak peek at the issues and ideas shared by real professional game designers, go online to these informative
Web sites. Just keep in mind that these are intended for
professionals—people who are really serious about computer
games.

☼ Game Week News at http://www.gignews.com
☼ Game Developer Net at http://www.gamedev.net

And for some excellent resources about breaking into the
computer game profession, go online to http://www.igda.
org/breakingin/home.htm.

AT THE LIBRARY

COMPUTERIZED CAREER CONSIDERATIONS

Get your nose in some of the following books to find out
more about what it's like to have a career in computer game
design.

Ferguson. *Careers in Focus: Computer and Video Game
Design*. New York: Ferguson, 2005.
———. *Discovering Careers for Your Future*. New York: Fer-
guson, 2001.
Firestone, Mary. *Weird Careers in Science: Computer Game
Developer*. Langhorne, Pa.: Chelsea House, 2005.
McGinty, Alice. *Cool Careers: Software Designer*. New York:
Rosen Publishing, 2000.
Olesky, Walter. *Cool Careers: Video Game Designer*. New
York: Rosen Publishing, 2000.

Just for fun, help the Boxcar children solve the computer game caper featured in:

Warner, Gertrude Chandler. *The Mystery of the Computer Game*. Morton Grove, Ill.: Albert Whitman and Company, 2000.

GET IN THE GAME

Are you ready to jump in and give computer-game design a try? The following books were written with young game designers in mind. Take a look and enlist the help of a favorite computer teacher or other grown-up computer expert if you need it.

Harbour, Jonathan. *Visual Basic Game Programming*. Boston: Course Technology PTR, 2004.

Perdew, Les. *Game Art for Teens*. Boston: Course Technology PTR, 2004.

———. *Game Design for Teens*. Boston: Course Technology PTR, 2003.

Sethi, Manesh. *Game Programming for Teens*. Boston: Course Technology PTR, 2003.

WITH THE EXPERTS

Gamasutra
600 Harrison Street, 6th Floor
San Francisco, CA 94107
http://www.gamasutra.com

International Game Developers Association
870 Market Street, Suite 1181
San Francisco, CA 94102
http://www.igda.org

GET ACQUAINTED

Will Wright, Computer Game
Designer

CAREER PATH

CHILDHOOD ASPIRATION: To
be an astronaut, architect, or pilot.

FIRST JOB: Never had a real
job.

CURRENT JOB: Chief designer
and director at Maxis Corporation.

A DIFFERENT KIND OF MODEL

Will Wright always loved models—model ships, model planes, and model tanks. He enjoyed learning about the machine he was building and putting together the model. So when he started using a computer—an Apple II, in 1980—he was delighted to discover that it was possible to build models inside the computer. In those days, computer games were very primitive, but Wright realized that games were really models, little toy worlds, and he taught himself to program so that he could build these little toy worlds. Instead of building toys with balsa wood or plastic, he began to build them with lines of computer code.

SIDETRACKED COLLEGE DEGREE

Wright spent five years in college—studying architecture, mechanical aviation, and various other subjects—but he never quite got around to finishing his degree. He became infatuated with computer games instead of his studies.

He learned to program on the Apple II but decided that wouldn't take him very far, because thousands of people could already program on the Apple II. When the Commodore 64 computer arrived on the scene late in 1981, he saw his chance to get in right at the start of a new computer market. He bought a Commodore 64 immediately, then locked himself away in a room for a few weeks.

He learned how to program it as quickly as he could; then he wrote a game, a "stupid" game, he says. It was called *Raid on Bungling Bay*. He sold it to a large software company—Broderbund—and the game sold reasonably well in the United States. Broderbund licensed the game to Nintendo in Japan, where it sold 700,000 copies! With the royalties from Nintendo in hand, Wright didn't need to look for a job; he could continue programming.

Raid on Bungling Bay is a game in which helicopters bomb islands. Wright discovered something interesting while writing this program; he enjoyed creating the islands much more than he enjoyed bombing them. He discovered that, for him at least, the research required to create the game was more fun than creating the game itself.

In 1985 he began work on a program called *SimCity*, a computer model of a city. In 1987 he met Jeff Braun at a pizza party and described the game he was working on. Together they founded Maxis, hired a small group of programmers, and published the game two years later. Since that time *SimCity* has sold over 5 million copies.

MILLIONS OF COPIES LATER . . .
Maxis has sold millions of copies of other Sim products: *SimEarth*, *SimAnt*, *SimCopter*, *SimTower*, and plenty more. These are far more than simple "shoot-em-up" games; they require a great deal of planning and research to create. In fact, Wright spent two years researching ants while working on *SimAnt*. These programs are models of real-world systems—cities, planets, colonies, and so on—and they incorporate basic artificial intelligence technology.

Wright does a little programming these days, but he has a staff of programmers to do the bulk of the work. "For me, the research is the best thing," he says. "I still like programming and it's essential that I still understand programming to a detailed level, but most of my time is spent in designing games."

Creating computer games can be tremendously stressful, but it can also be tremendously satisfying. Wright comments, "The hardest part, by far, is the last two months of a project; 90 percent of the effort is done in the last 10 percent of the time, getting the bugs out and finishing off details. You don't get much sleep during that time, but there's a great feeling of satisfaction when the product's finally out the door."

Computer Programmer

SHORTCUTS

GO visit a computer store and look at all the latest computer technology.

READ about how personal computers work at http://computer.howstuffworks.com/pc.htm.

TRY learning more about the history of computers at the Computer History Museum at http://www.computerhistory.org/timeline.

SKILL SET

✔ COMPUTERS

✔ MATH

✔ SCIENCE

WHAT IS A COMPUTER PROGRAMMER?

A computer programmer tells computers what to do by writing computer programs. The programmer sits down at a computer terminal and types in a set of instructions known as source code. Although source code may look like ordinary text that anyone with a word processing program could create, in reality it is very complex and very (make that very, very) specific in what it tells computers to do. The truth is, a computer without computer programs would be like a person without a brain. Programmers make computers smart by writing programs that do the thinking for them.

When the instructions are complete, the programmer compiles the program; that is, he uses a compiler program to take the text instructions and convert them into a program file, such as the .exe and .com files you see when you look in Windows File Manager or Windows Explorer. This is the file that actually does the work, the file that is sold to customers.

If you were to watch a computer programmer at work, it would seem that they were simply sitting in front of their computer terminal and typing. But they aren't typing ordinary words; they are typing commands using a programming language. There are hundreds of programming languages and, yes, they would seem as unfamiliar as a foreign language to the average person. You've probably heard of some of them: Visual Basic, FORTRAN, Pascal, BASIC, Assembly, C, C++, Java, and Ada. (Ada is named after Ada Lovelace, the world's first computer programmer, who, believe it or not, died in 1852. She created programs for Charles Babbage's analytical machine, which he never quite got around to building.) There are lots of different programs for many different purposes, and most programmers understand several languages.

In fact, most programmers learn several languages because they really enjoy it. This is not the sort of career to get into just because you need a way to make a living; it's a "love it or hate it" type of thing, and good programmers really love programming. Programmers generally find that they enjoy the creative process of building something from scratch, spending hours on end at the keyboard. On one hand, it can be very exciting and satisfying to watch a program develop on the screen. On the other hand, there's often a lot of drudgery involved with programming. Even the most enthusiastic programmers encounter some tasks that they dislike intensely, such as testing the program to get the bugs out of it or documenting the program so that other people can use it.

In one way, programming is often a team effort. Many projects involve hundreds of programmers handling very specific aspects of the overall program. In another way,

programming can also be a very solitary task: it's just the programmer and the computer. If you think you're more of a "people person," this may not be the job for you.

If you think you might enjoy programming, however, the only way to find out is by trying it. Take programming classes at school. Learn Logo at home or in the school computer lab (see under Artificial Intelligence Scientist and Computer Game Designer to find out how to obtain a copy of Logo). Try as many programming languages as you can.

Once you graduate from high school, you'll want to consider pursuing a computer science degree in college—that's probably the easiest way into the career. However, many very skilled and highly respected programmers have no degree or have a degree in a completely unrelated subject. This is the sort of career in which many people are self-taught.

Actually, once you start trying to learn how to program, the decision of whether or not to be a computer programmer will become pretty obvious. If you catch on fast, enjoy it, and find it difficult to tear yourself away from the computer, you'll know you've caught the programming bug.

 # TRY IT OUT

COMPUTER TIME WARP

Gordon Moore, founder of Intel, made a prediction back in 1965 that computing power would double every year. The time-frame was later extended to every 18 months, but the prediction has held true to this day. See what you can find out about how computers have changed (and improved!) over the years by checking out these Web sites about computer history:

- History of Computers at http://www.kidcompute. com/history.html
- Greatest Engineering Achievements of the Twentieth Century at http://www.greatachievements.org/?id=2956
- Computer History Museum at http://www. computerhistory.org
- Computer History from B.C. to Today at http:// www.computerhope.com/history

M. C. A. Library
3800 S. Fairview Road
Santa Ana, CA 92704
(714) 556-0965

☼ Evolution of the Computer at http://history.sandiego.
edu/gen/recording/computer1.html

Use what you discover to create a computer timeline that tells the story of computers in an interesting way.

PROGRAM DISSECTION

According to experts, computer programming is one of the fastest-growing professions around. Have you every wondered what all these newly employed programmers are doing? What about those projects that involve hundreds of programmers— what could all those people possibly be doing?

Good questions! Here's how to find some answers. First, go to a computer store and make a list of all the different kinds of programs that you find. Make a note of what each program is used for. Find one that looks particularly interesting or complicated and look on the back of the box for a toll-free phone number or an Internet address.

Call or e-mail the company and ask to be put in touch with one of the programmers. Tell them that you are interested in becoming a programmer some day and are trying to find out more about the profession. Ask them to describe how the team of programmers worked together to produce the program you are inquiring about. Find out how many different people were involved and what their roles were.

After your discussion, make a chart that illustrates the process. Highlight the part of the process in which you would have liked to have been involved.

If you happen to already know someone who's a programmer, you can ask them to help you with this project.

✔ CHECK IT OUT

🖱 ON THE WEB

PROGRAMMING FOR KIDS

Give computer programming a try at some of these Web sites that are mostly just for kids:

☼ Block Corner at http://www.blockcorner.com/content.html

- ☼ Games Basic at http://www.mathplayground.com/LogoProgramming.html
- ☼ Kids Can Program at http://www.hvac.cc/kidscanprogram/main/tofc.htm
- ☼ Kids Compute at www.kidcomputer.com
- ☼ Math Playground at http://www.mathplayground.com/LogoProgramming.html

KEYBOARD RACES

In the old days of the Wild West, cowboys who could draw their weapons the fastest were the ones most likely to survive. In today's computer frontier, computer programmers have to be fast on the draw with their keyboarding skills to keep pace with the demands of the job. Brush up your skills and enjoy some keyboard antics at the following Web sites:

- ☼ Computer Circus at http://library.thinkquest.org/18709/data/practice.html
- ☼ Word Games Typing Test at http://www.world-english.org/wordgames5.htm
- ☼ Letter Speed Game at http://www.freewebs.com/weddell/findtheletter.html
- ☼ TypeShark Game at http://www.popcap.com/launchpage.php?theGame=typershark&src=big8
- ☼ Type Me Game at http://games.funschool.com/game.php?g=arcade/typememenu&t=j&w=620&h=360

 AT THE LIBRARY

PROGRAMMER-TO-BE

These books will help you continue to weigh the pros and cons of becoming a computer programmer.

Bonnice, Sherry. *Careers With Character: Computer Programmer.* Broomall, Pa.: Mason Crest, 2003.

Henderson, Harry. *A to Z of Computer Scientists.* New York: Facts On File, 2003.

Marx, Christy. *Grace Hopper: The First Woman to Program the First Computer in the United States.* New York: Rosen Publishing, 2003.

Parks, Peggy J. *Exploring Careers: Computer Programming.* Farmington Hills, Mich.: KidHaven Press, 2003.

Wallner, Rosmary. *Career Exploration: Computer Programmer.* Minneapolis: Capstone Press, 2000.

WITH THE EXPERTS

Association of Information
Technology Professionals
401 North Michigan Avenue,
Suite 2400
Chicago, IL 60611-4267
http://www.aitp.org

Institute for Certification of
Computer Professionals
2350 East Devon Avenue, Suite
115
Des Plaines, IL 60018
http://www.iccp.org

GET ACQUAINTED

Victor Kushdilian, Computer Programmer

CAREER PATH

CHILDHOOD ASPIRATION: To be a scientist working in the space program.

FIRST JOB: Assistant to an electrical engineer, working on printed circuit board layout.

CURRENT JOB: President of SportsWare.

STARTING WITH HARDWARE

Victor Kushdilian always enjoyed math and science, so as a kid he thought he'd like to work on the space program. That's why he earned a degree in electrical engineering at the University of Southern California. However, his first job after graduating was not in engineering but with IBM (International Business Machines) as a computer technician. He worked on computer hardware for seven or eight years.

Large companies such as IBM often provide training opportunities for their employees, and Kushdilian made the most of it. He learned about systems software, operating systems, and mainframe programming. Eventually he began programming as part of his job.

He was also programming at home, just for fun. Kushdilian has always been a creative person. He enjoys building things and is often doing things around his house. He found that programming is just another form of creating something. You build a program, watch it grow, and see it come alive.

COMPUTERIZED FOOTBALL

He began by creating small database programs. A database program simply stores data in a structured form so that the data can be searched for and retrieved quickly. Many computer programs are essentially database programs—address books and contact managers, e-mail programs, mail-merge programs, and so on—and many others include some form of database. Working with databases is a good skill for a programmer to have.

A database needs data, of course, so Kushdilian found a favorite source of data he could use while experimenting with these programs: football statistics. He began by creating a database that would store football stats and allow him to find any piece of information he wanted. But then he took things a step further and created a fantasy football program. Fantasy football, played by millions of Americans, is a game in which players create make-believe teams using real players; that is, they pick the real-life players they'd like to have on their teams, then track each player's performance during the

game season. To do that, they have to collect a lot of information, and most people write down all this information on paper. But a computer database is an ideal tool for the job!

After writing the program for his own use, Kushdilian realized that if he found it useful, somebody else probably would too. So in 1990, almost on an impulse, he put an ad in a small football magazine offering copies of his program for $50. He got a few calls, but when he made his first sale, he really wasn't prepared. He wasn't set up to accept payments, do accounting, or ship programs. He ran out and bought an invoice book and some office supplies, made a diskette, and sent it out.

That ad sold 30 copies of the program over the first year. Kushdilian called all 30 customers and asked them how he could make the program even better. Then he set about improving the program by adding new functions. All along, he'd still been working at IBM, but in 1992 he borrowed a little money, quit his job, and started a full-fledged business.

KEEP MOVING

Today, his business has moved from developing and marketing computer software to Internet services. As technology is constantly changing, computer companies must adapt to new technologies or perish. Starting in 2000, Sportsware transformed itself into a Web technology company providing all of its services on the Internet at http://www.comissioneronline. com.

This meant updating technical skills, learning new software, and training in new technical platforms. Since 2000, there has been a nonstop effort to stay on top of new technologies that the market demands. Kushdilian says you can never sit still in the world of computer technology!

Hardware Engineer

WHAT IS A HARDWARE ENGINEER?

Behind all the glitzy graphics and amazing capabilities of the latest software is the hardware that makes it happen. And behind all the hardware are the engineers whose ideas and hard work have made it all possible.

All the exciting things you can do with a computer, such as simulate travel in space and chat with people around the world, are brought to you courtesy of hardware engineers who have created the tools that run the software. Computer hardware includes the "guts" of a computer—all the pieces that make a computer work its magic.

Hardware engineers can be found in every area of the computer business. They design the chips that are at the very heart of the computer as well as the processors that are doubling in speed every 18 months. They design the boards that the processors sit on, known as motherboards. They design disk drives, video screens, the big tape drives used by mainframe computers, the networking components used to connect different computers together, the CD-ROM drives, modems, keyboards, mice, printers, and scanners. The list goes on and on.

And the list continues to grow: machines that "print" models of machine components in 3-D (they create three-dimensional

Hardware Engineer

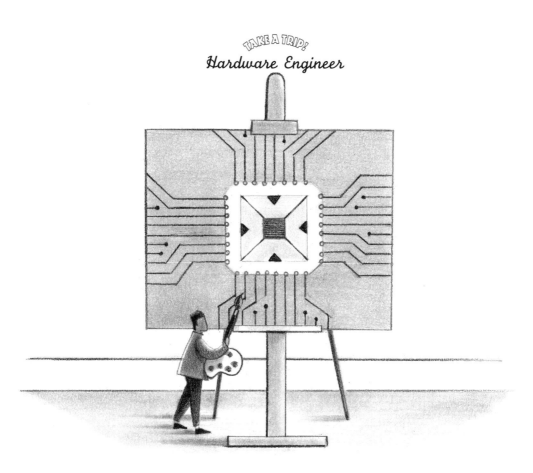

objects in a waxlike substance), machines that create smells, machines that print 3-D models of people's faces. These are all real technologies under development right now.

Hardware engineers have a wide range of roles. They are involved in the design of components at the very first level, creating the circuit diagrams that will be used to build the new component. They are also involved in development, building prototypes and modifying the item to get it to work properly. They're involved in testing the component; they make sure that the item will perform properly in any condition it's likely to work under, and they make sure that it's durable enough to last.

Hardware engineering is a very demanding career. There's an awful lot to learn, and an ability to apply advanced levels of math and science is required to do well in this career. You'll need a college degree in a subject such as electrical engineering. Many people in this business have advanced degrees too.

Not everyone who loves computers is cut out for this type of work. But for those who are, the rewards can be substantial—both in salary and job satisfaction. Hardware engineers are very well paid, and as it requires a lot of work to enter the profession, it seems likely that demand for hardware engineers will always be high.

If you are interested in becoming a hardware engineer, take all the math and science courses you can. If your school teaches electronics, study that too. You need to enjoy solving problems. Hardware engineering is like a very complicated puzzle, combining various components to create a new computer device. Math is an especially critical part of the job. So the better you are at math, the better you'll be as a hardware engineer.

 # TRY IT OUT

TRY A SCIENCE EXPERIMENT

Hardware engineers are creative scientists at heart. Cultivate that scientific mindset (and have a little fun) by conducting some of the experiments described in books such as:

Green, Joey. *Potato Radio, Dizzy Dice and More Wacky, Wild Experiments from the Mad Scientist.* New York: Perigree, 2004.
———. *Mad Scientist.* New York: Perigree, 2000.
———. *Mad Scientist II.* New York: Perigree, 2002.
Tymony, Cy. *Sneaky Uses for Everyday Things.* New York: Andrews McMeel, 2003.

 # CHECK IT OUT

🖱 ON THE WEB

HEADS-UP ABOUT NANOTECHNOLOGY

Hardware engineering is moving toward a really exciting technology: nanotechnology. In fact, nanotechnology is start-

ing to change the world of technology. Creating things is becoming very fast and very cheap, and we'll soon be able to create materials and products we can only dream of right now, such as microscopic robots that can move through a blood vessel seeking out viruses, and computers of a completely new type that are much faster and smaller than the ones we have today.

Visit a few nanotechnology Web sites and see what information is available. Perhaps one day you'll be working with this fantastic new technology.

You can link to all kinds of really cool nanotechnology Web sites for kids from the National Nanotech Initiative Web site at http://www.nano.gov/html/edu/eduk12.html.

HOW COMPUTERS WORK

Get acquainted with computer guts (more technically known as computer components) at the How Stuff Works Web site at http://www.howstuffworks.com. Once there, use the Web site's search engine to locate articles on bits and bytes, Boolean logic, microprocessors, modems, networking, and PCs.

GET TECH!

Find out about all kinds of high-tech opportunities at the Get Tech Web site, sponsored by the National Association of Manufacturers, at http://www.gettech.org.

AT THE LIBRARY

INSIDE SCOOP ON COMPUTER CAREERS

Read about careers of famous computer engineers as well as careers you can have in hardware engineering in books such as:

Brackett, Virginia. *Steve Jobs: Computer Genius of Apple.* Berkeley Heights, N.J.: Enslow, 2003.

Brashares, Ann. *Steve Jobs Thinks Different.* Brookfield, Conn.: Millbrook Press, 2001.

Donnelly, Karen. *Cool Careers: Hardware Engineer.* New York: Rosen Publishing, 2000.

Maupin, Melissa. *Computer Engineer.* Mankato, Minn.: Capstone Press, 2000.

Sherman, Josepha. *The History of the Personal Computer.* Danbury, Conn.: Franklin Watts, 2003.

IT'S GOT SOUL

For an idea of the excitement—and stress—involved in creating computer hardware, read *The Soul of a New Machine* by Tracy Kidder (Boston: Back Bay Books, 2000). Kidder watched a team of about 30 designers working for Data General in the 1970s create a new minicomputer, from the early designs to the finished product. Kidder made the story exciting—and won a Pulitzer Prize for his effort.

As you read, keep track of the phases the team went through from start to finish. See if you can identify all the steps between having a great idea and producing a working product.

WITH THE EXPERTS

IEEE Computer Society
1730 Massachusetts Avenue, NW
Washington, DC 20036-1992
http://www.computer.org

International Microelectronics and Packaging Society
611 2nd Street, NE
Washington, DC 20002
http://www.imaps.org/

Society of Manufacturing Engineers
International Headquarters
One SME Drive
Dearborn, MI 48121
http://www.sme.org

GET ACQUAINTED

John Pemberton, Hardware
Engineer

CAREER PATH

CHILDHOOD ASPIRATION:
To be an engineer after going
through the professional football
player phase.

FIRST JOB: Pumping gas and
fixing cars at a gas station
when he was a teenager.

CURRENT JOB: Manufacturing manager for a major
semiconductor company.

HIGH-TECH WORLD

John Pemberton works in a laboratory that operates 24 hours
a day, seven days a week. His staff consists of more than 500
technicians who work different shifts making computer chips.
He's responsible for more than $1 billion worth of equipment
and oversees a work environment that is 1,000 times cleaner
than a medical operating room. Everyone who enters the
super-sterile laboratory must wear head-to-toe gear known
as bunny suits. The technicians wear helmets so that even the
air they breathe is filtered.

The product being manufactured is so tiny that you can't
even see it without the help of a high-powered microscope.
Each technician works on a specific part of the process by
using very specialized tools. The entire process of manufacturing a computer chip takes about 50 to 60 days.

A JUGGLING ACT

When his sons ask him what he does at work, Pemberton likes
to tease them by saying he sits in meetings all day. As manager of the team that produces these high-tech components,

Pemberton certainly has lots of reasons to call a meeting. He says his work can be summed up in four words: productivity, planning, forecasting, and troubleshooting.

Productivity involves finding ways to make the most and best microchips with the least amount of resources. It means figuring out systems that are as quick and as efficient as possible.

Planning involves keeping things running smoothly and dealing with any number of issues that pop up when running an operation that involves hundreds of people and billions of dollars worth of high-tech equipment.

Forecasting is what keeps Pemberton's team one step ahead of the competition. He has to know how many chips to produce to keep the world's computers working in top condition.

Troubleshooting involves finding solutions to any problem that might hinder the successful production of microchips.

COLLEGE TO CAREER

Pemberton has actually worked for the same company ever since he graduated from college. He went to Iowa State University with the intention of becoming a chemical engineer. While there, he became interested in industrial engineering because of the way it combines engineering with management. He used his time in college to find out more about what he wanted in his career.

At an on-the-job learning experience at an antifreeze manufacturing factory, Pemberton discovered that he didn't want to do dirty work. Instead, he started looking for opportunities to work in a clean, environmentally friendly manufacturing setting. When he took some computer courses in college and really enjoyed them, he decided that the electronics industry might be just the place to start looking for his ideal job.

Right before he graduated, he sent résumés to various electronics companies. He received an offer from one of the industry "giants" but chose to join the up-and-coming firm he still works with now. It turned out to be a good choice for

Pemberton, as he's had plenty of opportunity to advance his career as a hardware engineer.

A JUMP START

Pemberton credits his father and grandfather with nurturing the skills he needed to be successful as an engineer. Pemberton's dad worked with him when he was a child, giving him help in math and problem-solving and teaching him how to apply mathematical principles to real-life situations. His grandfather, who worked in the heating and air-conditioning business, spent time with Pemberton, showing him how to build things and put things together. Through these experiences he gained an appreciation for the mechanical world and discovered how much he enjoyed it.

WORDS OF ADVICE

1. **Math**. Master it and you can do anything in engineering.

2. **Work**. Get a job while you're young and you'll discover some interesting things about yourself, the value of money, and your priorities in life.

3. **Learn**. Pay attention in high school. It's tough to make up for lost time in college.

Internet Systems Administrator

SHORTCUTS

GO visit some of the best Internet Web sites for kids at http://www.surfnetkids.com.

READ articles in the DK Google *e.Encyclopedia* (New York: DK Publishing, 2003) and visit the book's special Web site at http://www.dke-encyc.com.

TRY comparing popular Internet search engines such as Google (http://www.google.com), Yahoo (http://www.yahoo.com), and Netscape (http://www.netscape.com).

SKILL SET

✔ COMPUTERS
✔ SCIENCE
✔ MATH

WHAT IS AN INTERNET SYSTEMS ADMINISTRATOR?

The Internet is the new Wild West, and the systems administrators are the new sheriffs. Their job is to keep the Internet safe from computer viruses, cybercrooks, hackers, and technological snafus that constantly threaten the free flow of information around the world.

An Internet service provider (ISP) is a company that sells access to the Internet. America Online and CompuServe are large ISPs, but there are many thousands of small ISPs too. ISPs range from companies with just one or two employees to huge national or international companies with thousands of employees. The systems administrator's job is to keep the ISP's computers running and to make sure that the company's customers are able to connect to the Internet.

The systems administrator is therefore responsible for many things. The most important responsibility is keeping the

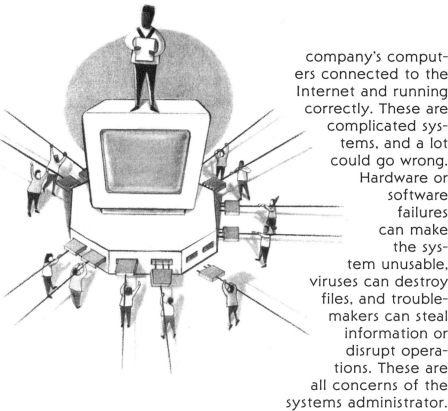

company's comput-
ers connected to the
Internet and running
correctly. These are
complicated sys-
tems, and a lot
could go wrong.
Hardware or
software
failures
can make
the sys-
tem unusable,
viruses can destroy
files, and trouble-
makers can steal
information or
disrupt opera-
tions. These are
all concerns of the
systems administrator.

The systems administrator is also responsible for upgrad-
ing equipment and installing new equipment as the company grows. It doesn't take long for computers and modems
to become out of date in this business. It seems as though
everybody in the entire industry replaces most of their
modems every 18 months or so.

There's more. The systems administrator may have to help
customers with their software configuration problems, especially if he or she is working for a small service provider (larger
companies have technical-support departments that handle this
sort of thing). Although much better now than just two or three
years ago, Internet-connection software is still tricky to configure in many cases, and in small companies the administrator
may spend a lot of time on the phone or perhaps even making
"house calls" to help customers get everything set up properly.
The administrator may also have to help large business customers set up their networks and perhaps provide training as well.

One of the most exciting parts of the job is battling computer break-ins. A computer cracker is someone who tries to break into other people's computers by exploiting the network link with the outside world. Someone sitting at a computer connected to the Internet in Germany, for example, can attempt to break into another Internet-connected computer in Mexico. A prime target is the Internet service provider's system. In many cases, crackers are just out to see how far they can get, just for fun. In some cases, they are carrying out malicious acts, intentionally damaging systems. And in other cases, they're using ISP systems as "way stations," places to store stolen software for a short time.

A skilled systems administrator can watch for break-ins and take steps to thwart the attacker's actions. The administrator may even be able to track down where the cracker is operating and then contact the administrator of the system being used by the cracker. Sometimes, a cat and mouse game begins as the administrator searches for the cracker and works to have the cracker thrown off the system. The cracker may then find another system and return, breaking in again. The battle is never quite won. The systems administrator is the sheriff of his or her system, and the sheriffs often work together—forming a posse, almost—to fight the bad guys on the Internet.

 # TRY IT OUT

FIND A NETWORK

You'll probably find it difficult to get your hands on the expensive equipment that Internet service providers use, but there are similarities among networks of all kinds. Does your school computer lab have a network? It probably has Internet access. Try to find out about all the connections.

Track down the school systems administrator or the computer teacher, and ask if you can spend some time watching him or her working on the network—installing network connections or modems, for instance, or configuring network software.

It's quite complicated stuff, but if you ask lots of questions, you may be able to pick up some of the jargon and basic networking concepts.

FIND A NETWORK

It may seem a little complicated at first, but as with most things related to computers, there's a logical reason for everything. After asking lots of questions, see if you can sketch out a simple diagram that illustrates your school's computer network system.

SAFE SURFING

The Internet is like a highway in that it is full of traffic, interesting detours, and fascinating destinations. It's also like a highway in that you've got to be careful when you venture out online. Imagine that you are the Internet systems administrator at your school. Make a colorful poster that explains how to stay safe online in a way that the younger kids at your school would understand. For ideas, go online to http://www.ikeepsafe.org/index.php.

✔ CHECK IT OUT

🖱 ON THE WEB
INTERNET SCHOOL

It didn't take long for the Internet to become an important part of life on planet Earth. People use it to find information, plan vacations, and keep in touch. You can even use it to learn more about it.

- ☀ For a crash course in the Internet, go online to http://www.internet101.org.
- ☀ Get up to speed on the latest instant messaging lingo at http://www.internet101.org/terms.html or http://www.noslang.com.
- ☀ When you want to goof around online, visit http://www.kids-online.net/kidsframe.html.

AT THE LIBRARY

DESTINATION INTERNET

Explore the World Wide Web in books that include:

Lewis, Ian. *How to Conquer the Internet*. Danbury, Conn.: Franklin Watts, 2002.

Rominger, Lynne. *Extraordinary Blogs And Ezines*. Danbury, Conn.: Franklin Watts, 2006.

Royston, Angela. *Internet and Email: In Touch*. Portsmouth, N.H.: Heinemann, 2001.

Sherman, Josepha. *History of the Internet*. Danbury, Conn.: Franklin Watts, 2003.

———. *Internet Safety*. Danbury, Conn.: Franklin Watts, 2003.

CRACK THE CODE

No matter what they are supposed to do, all computer programs and systems have at least one thing in common: codes. Whether making them or breaking them, Internet systems administrators often get cozy with codes. Here are some books that explore this fascinating world:

Janeczko, Paul. *Top Secret: A Handbook of Codes, Ciphers, and Secret Writing*. Cambridge, Mass.: Candlewick, 2005.

Singh, Simon. *The Code Book for Young People: How to Make It, Break It, Hack It, Crack It*. New York: Delacorte, 2002.

Wiess, Jim. *Spy Science: 40 Secret-Sleuthing, Code-Cracking, Spy-Catching Activities for Kids*. New York: Jossey Bass, 1996.

And, just for fun, join these fictional characters in cracking the code—before it's too late:

Balliett, Blue. *Chasing Vermeer*. New York: Scholastic, 2005.

🗣️ WITH THE EXPERTS

Association for Computer Machinery
1515 Broadway
New York, NY 10036
http://www.acm.org

SANS (SysAdmin Audit Network Security) Institute
8120 Woodmont Avenue, Suite 205
Bethesda, MD 20814
http://www.sans.org

Systems Administrators Guild
USENIX Association
2560 Ninth Street, Suite 215
Berkeley, CA 94710
http://sageweb.sage.org

GET ACQUAINTED

Rachel Drummond, Internet
Systems Administrator

CAREER PATH

CHILDHOOD ASPIRATION: To be a marine biologist, firefighter, welder, or physicist. She never realized that anyone could use computers to make a living.

FIRST JOB: Receptionist at Expert Internet Service.

CURRENT JOB: Systems administrator.

WORKING HER WAY UP THE LADDER

Rachel Drummond has loved computers for a long time. She first programmed her Atari 800 when she was 10, making it play violin music. She'd always hoped her parents would buy her a bigger, more powerful computer, but she probably lost that chance when she set the Atari to play a mind-numbing music loop and turned the volume up full blast for hours on end.

She was 22 before she got her next computer, which she used to connect to GEnie, an online service. Drummond was launching a short-story magazine named Sequitur and started a discussion group on GEnie to promote the magazine.

While in high school, Drummond attended classes in the school district's career enrichment center, where they offered bricklaying classes, beautician classes, and computer classes. The center had a big mainframe computer, and Drummond learned how to program in Assembly, BASIC, and FORTRAN.

HOOKED ON THE INTERNET

After college, where she studied engineering and physics, she found herself unemployed and looking for a job, but she stayed connected to the Internet for hours at a time, reading news group messages and using role-playing games such as MUDs (Multi-User Dungeons) and MUSHes (Multi-User Shared Hallucinations). In those days, 1994, Internet access was expensive, and Drummond couldn't afford to pay the eight hours she was online each day. So she called her Internet service provider and offered to trade some part-time work in return for online time. She started working at Expert Internet Service as the receptionist.

While working as the receptionist, she discovered main pages. These are the online documents that explain UNIX programs, and Drummond began reading all she could find. The more she read, the more she learned. Of course, as she was receptionist, she often answered calls from customers who had problems. Since her boss couldn't keep up with all the calls, Drummond started tackling some of them herself.

Soon her boss realized that she knew more about some subjects than he did, and he would pass questions on to her. Eventually he realized that she could answer most customer questions better than he could, so he gave her the systems administrator job.

THE THRILL OF THE CHASE

Drummond loves keeping up on technology because there's so much to learn. She especially loves the constant variety. She also enjoys having to solve the problems that occur when equipment is malfunctioning. But the part of the job she loves most is chasing people!

She chases spammers (people sending huge amounts of unwanted e-mail across the Internet) and gets their Internet accounts closed, and she chases people who abuse the Expert Internet Service computer system. "I feel like someone's broken into my house!" she says. "I get furious, very protective, and I'm not going to let them get away with it."

Drummond is partly responsible for the very first prosecution of an Internet software pirate. The cracker broke into the Expert Internet Service system, created hidden directories, and then stored over 600 MB of "cracked" software (that is, computer programs that have been modified so that they can be used without a registration number). This is a common trick used by software pirates. They store files on a computer that they've broken into—hoping that the administrator hasn't noticed—and then tell other people that they can go to the site to download the software. Only this time, this system administrator did notice.

In conjunction with the Software Publishers Association, Drummond began tracking the cracker's actions. She was able to track him back to his Internet access point, and eventually he was caught by the police in San Francisco. Unfortunately, he jumped bail and traveled up and down the West Coast before being caught again in Seattle.

ONE THING LEADS TO ANOTHER

When you work as a systems administrator in a Unix system, the logic and organization becomes second nature. In Unix, you have the opportunity to actually know what's going on with the machine, right from the start. It's all open and the only "black boxes" are the ones that you choose not to open. Other operating systems go to great lengths to hide their workings from the user.

According to Drummond, as you move into other computer fields, you bring with you a knowledge of computer architecture and software behavior that is applicable to everything you do. When she's testing scientific ideas, it's useful to know how the computer encodes the theoretical language of math and science into finite approximations of reality. And, speaking of testing scientific ideas, Drummond is busy doing that very thing as she pursues a master's degree in applied mathematics in computational biology.

She hopes to combine her love of math and computers to explore biomimetics. Biomimetics, she explains, involves studying how nature does things so that manufacturers can mimic certain processes to make products for humans. For instance, she's been busy looking at spider webs and has discovered that the silk they use to spin their webs is stronger than the Kevlar material used to make bullet-proof vests. Drummond said that if scientists can figure out the amino acid sequence of a spider's silk, they might one day be able to make a similar strand that could in turn be used to make bulletproof T-shirts. How cool is that!

COMPUTER CENTRAL

In addition to using computers to make a living, Drummond says that computers are a huge part of everyday life for her family (including a husband she met while playing an online game, their two sons, and a soon-to-be-adopted daughter from China). She uses computers to enhance her hobby as a digital photographer, to showcase her photos on a blog, and even to preplan the designs she uses in making quilts. You can find out more about Drummond and see some of her photography at http://macromath.blogspot.com.

Multimedia Developer

SHORTCUTS

GO visit a computer store that has demo software running and spend time playing with the best multimedia programs they have available.

READ about the history of multimedia at http://www.artmuseum.net/w2vr/timeline/timeline.html.

TRY using all the graphics and animation software you can find at school, home, or the library.

WHAT IS A MULTIMEDIA DEVELOPER?

You've seen multimedia in computer games, CD encyclopedias and books, and on the World Wide Web. It involves a creative blend of graphics, animation, video, and text to provide information and entertainment in an interactive computer environment. Good multimedia is very expensive and complicated to create, so it takes a team of people to do the many required tasks.

Producing a multimedia product is comparable to making a movie. In the film business, you have actors, artists, camera operators, makeup people, and directors. Multimedia developers are the directors of the multimedia business. They steer the multimedia project in the right direction, ensuring that everyone involved is moving toward the same goal.

Who else is involved in a multimedia project? That depends on what's going into the project. Almost all multimedia projects have artists and writers, the people who create the pictures and text. They also have programmers, who take all the words and pictures and put them into the multimedia program. The artists may also be involved in creating animation,

although some projects require an animation specialist. Voice "talent" (actors who provide vocals for the project) may be required; in many small multimedia projects, however, the voices are provided by the artists, writers, developers, and other staff. More sophisticated projects involve professional actors as well.

The multimedia developer runs the show and plans the overall project. Two tasks are at the heart of the developer's job: designing the look and feel of the product and managing the overall project. Although the developer may also be part of the creative team, he or she manages the project by delegating tasks, scheduling goals, and making sure that these goals are met.

Although computer multimedia has been around for awhile, for a long time it was more promise than reality, more hype than truth.

But, in the last few years, multimedia capabilities have improved by leaps and bounds. Even personal computers now have the power to handle many of the "bells and whistles" of a full-fledged multimedia program. Internet bandwidth allows for the quick and reliable transfer of incredible amounts of information. And sophisticated programming languages like Java now allow for easy access to sound, music, and video clips on the Web. It's all just a click of the mouse away.

Games and 3-D animation are getting pretty close to awesome these days. They are interactive, more realistic, and getting better all the time.

More and more colleges are offering programs in multimedia as businesses, the entertainment world, and education are finding uses for multimedia products and platforms. A good program will emphasize both the technical and creative aspects of multimedia as you'll need a firm grasp of both to succeed in this field.

If you are interested in this field, you can start by visiting as many cool Web sites as you can find, playing as many computer games as your schedule will allow, and taking as many computer and graphics courses as you can handle. How's that for a fun homework assignment?

☞ TRY IT OUT

GO INTERACTIVE

As with many things in life, the best way to find out if you like working with multimedia is to just do it. There are a couple ways to do this. One way is to go online to a variety of Web sites and see how they use different kinds of media to enlighten and entertain. Another way is to experiment with different kinds of software for kids and pay attention to how they do what they do. Your school computer center or public library may provide free access to a variety of programs. Still another way is to ask your parents about purchasing a graphic design or animation software package for your home computer. A variety of programs are available just for kids.

Take a look at the options at your local computer store or do some online shopping at Amazon (http://www.amazon.com) using the Web site's search engine to look for "graphic design software for kids."

Make up a chart where you can compare some of the features of the programs and Web sites you explore. You'll want to take note of things such as how easy (or not) the programs are to use, how appealing they look, how interesting they are to play with, and so on.

SENSORY STORYTELLING

In the simplest of terms, multimedia involves telling stories using words, pictures, and sound. Put all three ingredients together by retelling one of your favorite childhood stories using—you got it—words, pictures, and sound. For a high-tech version, you can use Microsoft PowerPoint. Or go low-tech if you must, using paper, markers, and a tape recorder or radio for sound.

✔ CHECK IT OUT

🖱 ON THE WEB

GO TO CYBER SCHOOL

Teach yourself some multimedia smarts by learning all you can at some of the following Web sites:

- 💡 Find some helpful animation and multimedia tutorials at Kid's Rule at http://accessarts.org/ArtKids/Tutorials/Animation.
- 💡 Check out the latest and greatest in cool kids' Web sites at http://yahooligans.yahoo.com/content/cool.
- 💡 Explore the history of computer animation at http://www.bergen.org/AAST/ComputerAnimation.
- 💡 Learn the ropes of 2D and 3D animation at http://www.kidzonline.org/TechTraining.
- 💡 See how Web animation works at http://computer.howstuffworks.com/web-animation.htm.

☼ Get the skinny on multimedia at http://en.wikipedia. org/wiki/Multimedia.

BEST IN THE BUSINESS
When it comes to creating multimedia movies, shows, and Web sites, nobody does it better than Hollywood. Check out the latest multimedia adventures of these kid-pleasing companies:

☼ Disney (home to Mickey, Donald, and a slew of first-rate multimedia productions) at http://www.disney.com
☼ Nickelodeon (creators of *Blue's Clues*, *Dora the Explorer*, and *Sponge Bob Squarepants*) at http://www.nick.com
☼ Pixar (producers of favorites such as *Toy Story*, *Monsters, Inc.*, and *The Incredibles*) at http://www.pixar. com

 AT THE LIBRARY
READ ALL ABOUT IT

Caplin, Steve. *Max Pixel's Adventures in Adobe Photoshop Elements* 3. Berkeley, Calif.: Adobe Press, 2005.
Parks, Peggy J. *Computer Animator*. Farmington Hills, Mich.: Kidhaven Press, 2005.
Perry, Robert L. *Multimedia Magic*. Danbury, Conn.: Franklin Watts, 2000.
Souter, Gerry, Janet Souter, and Allison Souter. *Bringing Photos, Music, and Video to Your Web Page*. Berkeley Heights, N.J.: Enslow Publishers, 2003.
———. *Creating Animation for Your Web Page*. Berkeley Heights, N.J. Enslow Publishers, 2003.

 WITH THE EXPERTS
Association for Applied Interactive Multimedia
http://www.aaim.org

Association for Multimedia Communications
PO Box 10645
Chicago, IL 60610
http://www.amcomm.org

National Alliance for Media Arts and Culture
145 Ninth Street, Suite 205
San Francisco, CA 94103
http://www.namac.org

GET ACQUAINTED

Art Roche, Multimedia Developer

CAREER PATH

CHILDHOOD ASPIRATION: To be a cartoonist.

FIRST JOB: Grocery story clerk.

CURRENT JOB: Creative director of the new media division at Cartoon Network.

Cartoons have been a way of life for Art Roche since he was a kid. He grew up in Orlando, Florida, and recalls always taking one art class or another. He took his first class in cartooning when he was about 11 and was hooked from there. He started drawing his own comic strips in middle school and high school.

When it came time to go to college, he decided to major in fine arts, with an emphasis in drawing and painting. But, even so, cartoons were still a main focus of his art, and he and a friend drew a daily comic strip at the University of Georgia.

Once he graduated, he wasn't sure how to make a living with art, so he started working in art galleries and, at one point, put together enough of his own artwork for a show. By the mid-1980s, he was ready to get a little more "practical" with his art and took some graphic design courses. At the time, computers were just starting to be used as a design tool.

A GRAPHIC CAREER MOVE

Next came what Roche's describes as his "first real job" as graphic artist for a Florida newspaper. There he was responsible for creating the maps, charts, illustrations, and cartoons that spiced up the paper's news and feature stories. This was also where he started using computers to do his job, even though he was pretty much on his own to learn how to use them since no one else in the newsroom had any computer experience either.

After getting married and moving to Atlanta, Roche worked for another newspaper, where he eventually moved up to be chief graphics artist. When the newspaper went out of business, it was time to move in a new direction as a freelance magazine designer.

CARTOONS REDISCOVERED

In spite of the real-life interruptions of growing up and making a living, cartoons were still the art form that Roche most enjoyed. One of the benefits of living in Atlanta was that it put Roche in reach of the Turner Broadcasting Network, a media company that produces shows such as CNN and the Cartoon Network. Roche's freelance work eventually got him to the door of the Turner Production Studio Design Group on a part-time basis. But it was his computer design expertise that turned the freelance work into a full-time job where Roche worked his way up to art director of motion picture graphic design.

It was his ongoing love affair with cartons that eventually landed him a spot at the Cartoon Network. Talk about a dream job! According to Roche, the job has proven to be a perfect fit. Even though he's not "doing cartoons," he's involved with them every day, and, from his point of view, work just doesn't get much better than that.

His job as creative director of new media is to build exciting Web sites that support the cartoons featured round the clock on Cartoon Network. If the number of people who visit the Web site is any indication—9 to 10 million "unique" visitors per month—Roche is doing a great job. Roche's design staff of 55 use their skills as flash programmers, flash designers, writers, and Web developers to introduce each show's characters, generate interest in upcoming episodes, and create fun online games.

MULTIMEDIA MOGUL IN TRAINING

Roche says there are a few things you can start doing now to prepare for a career like his. Since his work involves equal measures (more or less) of artistic creativity, story-telling, and technology, he recommends seeking experiences and classes in all three areas.

In the meantime, you can join in Roche's multimedia adventures by visiting the Cartoon Network Web site at http://www.cartoonnetwork.com or kick-start your cartoon training by reading both of Roche's books:

Art for Kids: Cartooning. Asheville, N.C.: Lark, 2005.
Art for Kids: Comic Strips. Asheville, N.C.: Lark, 2006.

Online Researcher

SHORTCUTS

GO volunteer at your public or school library. Learn as much as possible about how the librarians find the answers to people's questions.

READ some of the great homework resources found at http://www.kidinfo.com.

TRY going online to look for the origin and meaning of your name.

WHAT IS AN ONLINE RESEARCHER?

An online researcher is someone who looks for answers to questions. Many different types of companies employ researchers to find the information they need to do business. Law firms, for example, need to research legal precedent, meaning they need to find earlier legal cases that have a bearing on cases the firm is currently handling. Brokerage companies research investments, and companies that design high-tech products research competing products. Also, drug companies look for research that relates to new drugs they are developing. Finding answers to questions such as these can be challenging.

Researchers look for the answers in many different places. Among them are special databases—both those stored on compact disks and those available online. These databases are not the kind that just anyone can find on the Internet. Instead, they tend to be pay-as-you-search business databases such as Dialog, LexisNexis, and Dow Jones. These online databases, systems that have huge quantities of valuable business information, have been around for years. Lexis-Nexis claims that it adds almost 10 million documents each week.

With hundreds of millions of documents stored in databases around the world, how is it possible to find just the one you need? A well-trained and competent researcher knows where to look for the information or, at least, how to figure out where to look. It's not just a matter of typing a few key words into a search program and clicking a button. The researcher must understand what sort of information is likely to be found in which database. And even then, researching a single question may be a long, drawn-out process, with each little piece of information leading to another. Research is often like solving a mystery: you follow all the clues you can find and stay in hot pursuit of the ultimate answer.

In addition to using high-tech resources such as these databases, most researchers become exceptionally good at tracking down information on the Internet as well as in more traditional formats such as microfiche or paper directories.

Most researchers work for large companies, often in corporate libraries. But there's great potential in this career for starting your own business. A research firm can be set up with a relatively small investment. Many experienced researchers quit their jobs and go into business for themselves.

If you think you might be interested in a career as an online researcher, consider getting a degree in library science as a

starting point. Although a degree isn't essential, it's certainly very helpful. A liberal-arts education can be very useful too. For instance, an English degree with lots of electives provides a broad-based education. While many researchers have a specialty—medicine or business, for example—a very broad range of knowledge helps the researcher find connections in information.

As a student, you may have already had a chance to test your research abilities while working on a term paper or class project. If you enjoyed the process of tracking down information and organizing it for a presentation, you'll want to consider the possibility of making this part of your future career.

 TRY IT OUT

TOP TEN

Pick a topic you'd like to know more about. It can be anything from chocolate to caterpillars as long as it's something you are really and truly interested in. Then go online and use popular (and powerful) search engines such as Google (http://www.google.com), Yahoo (http://www.yahoo.com), and Ask For Kids (http://www.askforkids.com) to research the topic until you find out 10 new facts about it that you didn't know before. When you are finished, make a poster to share your newfound wealth of knowledge.

CLIMB YOUR FAMILY TREE

Here's a project to put your research skills to the test and to put you in touch with your family roots. Go back in time and find out all you can about your ancestors.

To get started, go online to the Climbing Your Family Tree Web site at http://www.workman.com/familytree. There you'll find links to helpful resources, ideas and instructions, and a variety of downloadable activity sheets that will help you trace your family's roots.

✔ CHECK IT OUT

🖱 ON THE WEB

INTERNET DETECTIVE

Investigate some of the following Web research sites:

- ☆ Get into the research zone at http://www.classzone. com/books/research_guide.
- ☆ Learn how to research like a journalist at http:// nilesonline.com/data.
- ☆ Get your Web license at http://pbskids.org/license.
- ☆ Visit the kid's computer room at http://www. chirpingbird.com/netpets/html/computer/computer. html.
- ☆ And find a warm welcome to the Web at http:// www.actden.com/IE5.

HOMEWORK HELPERS

Get an edge on your homework—especially when your teacher assigns a research paper—at some of these informative Web sites for kids:

- ☆ Fact Monster at http://www.factmonster.com
- ☆ FirstGov for Kids at http://www.kids.gov/ k_homework.htm
- ☆ Homework Spot at http://www.homeworkspot.com
- ☆ National Geographic Homework Help at http:// www.nationalgeographic.com/education/homework
- ☆ Yahooligans Ask An Expert at http://yahooligans. yahoo.com/school_bell/ask_an_expert/

📚 AT THE LIBRARY

SEEK AND YE SHALL FIND

Expand your Internet horizons with some of the research tips found in the following books:

Pederson, Ted. *How to Find Almost Anything on the Internet.* Minneapolis: Sagebrush, 2001.

Souter, Gerry, Janet Souter, and Allison Souter. *Researching on the Internet Using Search Engines, Bulletin Boards, and Listservs.* Berkeley Heights, N.J.: Enslow Publishers, 2003.

Wolinsky, Art. *Internet Power Research Using the Big 6 Approach.* Berkeley Heights, N.J.: Enslow Publishers, 2002.

WITH THE EXPERTS

American Society for Information Science and Technology
1320 Fenwick Lane, Suite 510
Silver Spring, MD 20910
http://www.asis.org

Association of Independent Information Professionals
8550 United Plaza Boulevard, Suite 1001
Baton Rouge, LA 70809
http://www.aiip.org

GET ACQUAINTED

Amelia Kassel, Online Researcher

CAREER PATH

CHILDHOOD ASPIRATION: To be a ballet dancer.

FIRST JOB: Worked in a toy factory.

CURRENT JOB: President of MarketingBase, an online research company for businesses.

Amelia Kassel has a long history of chasing down answers to unusual questions. It all started back when she was a single teen mom with two children to raise. She had to find a "real" career that would support her growing family and decided to follow through with her sister's suggestion of going to college to be a librarian.

After graduating with a master's degree in library science, her career was officially launched at a biomedical library at the University of California–Los Angeles. A few years later, when her family moved to a location that didn't have a medical library, she accepted a position as an adult reference librarian in a public library. One of her main duties there was to help library customers find answers to questions that ranged from really easy, such as "where can I find a book about zoo animals," to the really weird, such as "what is the point gap for tuning up my 1955 Chevy." Kassel found the answer to the second question in an automotive repair manual. Ten years later, with the Internet just starting to take off, she was more than qualified to work as an information broker and started her own research company.

GOOGLE AND BEYOND

These days Amelia Kassel knows two things very well—the Internet and business. Both areas of expertise come into play when she works with clients to help them get ready to launch new products or to get an edge on their competitors. Kassel says that clients come to her to find information that they either can't find or don't have time to find themselves.

In some ways, Kassel is like a detective. But instead of tracking down criminals, she tracks down information. While she often starts her searches by "googling" for information like you do using Internet search engines such as http://www.google.com, she also uses a variety of fancy (and sometimes expensive) commercial databases that aren't available to the general public.

She's discovered that one skill in particular sets professional online researchers apart from amateurs: terminology. Figure

out the right words to describe what you are looking for and you are much more likely to find it, Kassel advises.

AN EXPERT'S EXPERT

In addition to helping business clients with their research needs, Kassel is a nationally recognized author and speaker about online research. She is a professor of library and information science at San Jose State University, has written a book called *The Super Searchers on Wall Street* (Medford, N.J.: *Information Today*, 2000), and is a regular speaker at conferences. In addition, she started a successful online training program for information brokers to train other people to do what she does. Along the way, she was pleasantly surprised to discover that she is a natural educator and enjoys sharing her expertise to help others.

Repair Technician

SKILL SET

✔ COMPUTERS

✔ SCIENCE

✔ BUSINESS

SHORTCUTS

GO to your local computer store to ask if you can visit the repair technicians "behind the scenes." Watch them at work for a little while and ask what they're doing.

READ *How to Build Your Own PC: Save a Buck and Learn A Lot* by Charlie Palmer (West Saint Paul, Minn.: HCM Publishing, 2005).

TRY installing a software program on a computer at school or at home. Follow the instructions very carefully.

WHAT IS A REPAIR TECHNICIAN?

You may have noticed by now that computers require lots of attention and maintenance. There always seems to be something going wrong with them: perhaps the modem you installed a few weeks ago isn't working properly, or you installed one program and now another has stopped working. Computers are very complicated, which is good news for computer repair technicians. There are plenty of problems to fix! You might think of repair technicians as the plumbers of the computer world. Just as when the water pipes burst, when a computer malfunctions, most people don't know what to do and must rely on the expertise of a professional who does. And, just as with plumbers, people pay their computer repair technicians a lot for their services and expertise.

The first part of any repair job requires troubleshooting or figuring out what's wrong. A computer problem can be caused by either hardware or software. A repair technician may have to use special programs to restore lost data or may have to replace a malfunctioning part. Other frequent software problems include cleaning up a computer's configuration settings to get things to run properly. And some

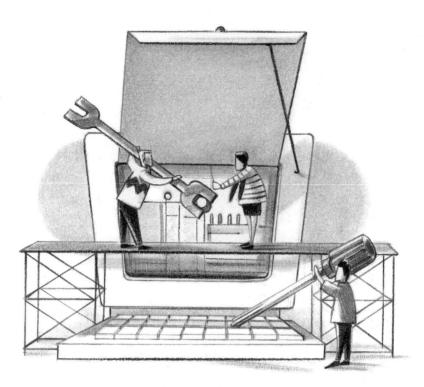

customers even pay to have software installed, to make sure it's done right.

Hardware problems can be just as varied. Hard disks are sometimes physically damaged by an electrical surge or by being dropped, and a repair technician will try to retrieve the data left on the disk. Computer screens often stop working, power supplies fail, or random access memory (RAM) sometimes acts up. All these problems can be fixed by the repair technician.

There's no established educational route for this job. There is a variety of certification programs created by some of the large software companies, such as Microsoft and Novell. A number of colleges have courses on computer repair. Far more important than a particular body of knowledge is a particular aptitude. You need to be persistent and a good problem-solver who can find solutions by drawing on experience as well as by trial and error. Because there's such a wide range of hardware and software products, you can never learn everything. What you can do, however, is to get a feel for problems and what might be causing them.

If you're interested in a career as a computer technician, take some high school electronics classes. While in high school, you might also try to get a part-time job working in a computer retail store; what you'll learn about computer products and jargon will help tremendously. You might also take community college courses on computer repair and maintenance.

Once you've learned the ropes, you'll find plenty of opportunity awaiting a skilled repair technician in computer stores, in electronic repair shops, or as an independent businessperson.

 TRY IT OUT

PLAY WITH A VOLTMETER

A basic tool of the repair technician is the voltmeter. A voltmeter is used to check voltages and other electrical characteristics such as circuit continuity (that is, to see if an electrical circuit is broken or is continuous). Someone at your school almost certainly has one; ask the science teacher.

With a little help and some supervision from a trusted adult, try a few things. Check the voltage on small batteries, C- or D-size batteries for instance. And see how the device can check circuit continuity by touching the contacts on the ends of a single wire. Try other substances to see if an electrical charge can flow through them: touch each side of a coin, different sides of a computer case, different sides of a filing cabinet, and so on. Checking for circuit continuity is an important technique for the repair technician, because broken circuits mean electrical signals no longer get through.

Create a chart to keep track of your discoveries.

TAKE A PEEK

Ask the computer teacher or your parent if you can take a look inside a computer. Make sure that the computer is unplugged and that an adult is supervising. Try to identify all the different components. Use the computer manual to double-check your guesses.

Start by identifying the components that can be accessed from the outside: the floppy and CD drives and the printer, serial, and telephone line ports at the back. Look for the hard drives too. See how these components are connected to the motherboard, the large computer board inside the computer. You should be able to see the power supply, a big box tucked away in one corner of the computer case.

Then try to identify the other components on the board: the memory chips, the processor, the small battery that keeps the computer's clock going, and the little jumper switches used to configure the computer's settings. Also try to identify any boards plugged into the motherboard: the modem, floppy drive controller, SCSI card, and so on.

Before you finish, make a diagram of what you see—being very careful to label each component correctly. Be careful not to touch anything! Static electricity from your fingers can damage sensitive electronic components.

BUILD IT AND IT WILL COMPUTE?

Good repair technicians know computers inside and out. See if you've got the right stuff by using items you find around the house or classroom to build your own "virtual" computer. Start with a cardboard box and use poster board, construction paper, or other items to create each component and tape or glue it in place.

✔ CHECK IT OUT

🖱 ON THE WEB
COMPUTER NEWS

Get up close and personal with the inner workings of computers by exploring information found at the following Web sites:

- ☼ Learn how all kinds of computer stuff works at http://computer.howstuffworks.com.
- ☼ Learn some computer basics on Fact Monster at http://www.factmonster.com/ipka/AO774696.html.

- ☼ Visit the Intel Museum at http://www.factmonster. com/ipka/AO774696.html.
- ☼ Click and see what's inside a computer at http:// www.kids-online.net/learn/c_n_l.html.
- ☼ Find out what's in the box at http://members.aol. com/wbox/wbox.htm.

AT THE LIBRARY

ELECTRONIC ESCAPADES

Many a computer repairperson got their start tinkering with electronics. Get a jump start on this career and have some fun doing some of the electronic experiments and projects described in these books:

Barthlomew, Alan. *Electronic Mischief: Battery Powered Gadgets Kids Can Build*. Tonawanda, N.Y.: Kids Can Press, 2002.

Columbo, Luann. *First Electronics: Smart Lab*. Bellevue, Wash.: Becker and Mayer, 2005.

Glover, David. *Batteries, Bulbs and Wires*. New York: Kingfisher, 2002.

McQuinn, Conn. *Electronics Lab*. Bellevue, Wash.: Becker and Mayer, 2005.

Stillinger, Doug. *Battery Science: Make Widgets that Work and Gadgets that Go*. Palo Alto, Calif.: Klutz, 2003.

WITH THE EXPERTS

Electronics Technicians Association-International
5 Depot Street
Greencastle, IN 46135
http://www.eta-i.org

International Society of Certified Electronics Technicians
3608 Pershing Avenue
Fort Worth, TX 76107
http://www.iscet.org

GET ACQUAINTED

Mike Little, Repair Technician

CAREER PATH

CHILDHOOD ASPIRATION: To do anything involved with new technologies.

FIRST JOB: Computer programmer.

CURRENT JOB: Owner of Techs-On-Call.

THANKS, RADIO SHACK!

When personal computers first arrived on the scene, in the late 1970s, Mike Little found them fascinating. He also found them expensive. In those days, schools didn't have computers, but Radio Shack did. In fact, Radio Shack was really the only place at the time where you could find computers that were accessible to kids. So Little would spend as much time as he could playing with the computers in his local mall's Radio Shack. He could sometimes stay as long as two hours before the staff would throw him out (which was occasionally long enough to create password programs to lock the staff out of their own computers).

Little taught himself BASIC programming in Radio Shack, working with primitive personal computers such as Radio Shack's TRS-80. He just sat down, read the manuals, and tried out everything he learned.

COLLEGE ON THE BEACH

When he was 19, Little went to Pepperdine University, in Malibu, California, just a couple of blocks from the beach. There he studied computer science and learned more about programming. When he finished college, he took a job as a programmer with a company creating a spreadsheet program. He soon discovered that even programmers have to experiment with hardware. The company he worked for seemed to run into more hardware problems than software problems, so Little soon learned the skills needed to keep computers running.

Little left this job after about a year and decided to take it easy for a while. He took on mainly part-time jobs, but he kept running into people who needed computers fixed, networks set up, or software installed. He found himself spending more and more time fixing things. No longer was he just doing a job long enough to make money to survive or to go on vacation; there was so much work finding him that it was turning into a full-time occupation.

TECHS-ON-CALL IS BORN

"No matter where I went or what I was doing, I ended up fixing people's computers," says Little. "'Hey I've got this computer problem,' people would say to me at parties. 'What do I do?' It was getting ridiculous, so I decided it was time to get serious."

In 1993 he got a business license and started Techs-On-Call. Since then his business has doubled each year. "I wake up every day thanking Bill Gates," he says. "He keeps me in business." Techs-On-Call now employs several people. They fix computers, of course, but they also install networks and cabling, install software and fix software problems, and just recently got into the business of setting up World Wide Web pages.

Two things make Little's business stand out in the world of computer repair. First, his company makes "house calls." Most companies make the customer bring the computer to them, but Little's company brings the tech to the computer—a very convenient service for many busy people.

Also, Little's employees are trained to be responsive on the human level, a trait often missing in computer experts. His technicians talk to clients, explaining what they are doing and why and exactly how much it will cost. "When people call you with computer problems, they're frantic. They're losing time or maybe even data," Little says. "You have to have an extraordinary amount of patience with them, to talk with them and tell them just what has to be done to fix their problems."

Software Entrepreneur

SHORTCUTS

GO online to the Entrepreneur Kids Web site at http://ww.entrepreneurkids.org.

READ *Beyond the Lemonade Stand* by Bill Rancic (New York: Razorbill, 2005).

TRY pitching in for a school fund-raiser to put your entrepreneurial spirit to work.

SKILL SET

✔ COMPUTERS

✔ BUSINESS

✔ TALKING

WHAT IS A SOFTWARE ENTREPRENEUR?

A software entrepreneur is someone in the business of developing and selling his or her own software. The great thing about this business is that it's still possible for a single person to come up with a good idea, write a program, and sell it.

You probably already know of at least one software entrepreneur: Bill Gates, the founder of Microsoft. But there are thousands more, from people who've made a comfortable living selling their own software to people who've become multimillionaires. In fact, we've already highlighted other entrepreneurs in this book: Will Wright (the cofounder of Maxis—see Computer Game Designer) and Victor Kushdilian (owner of SportsWare—see Computer Programmer).

In the early days of the personal computer, it was relatively easy for a software entrepreneur to get started. There were so few people involved at the beginning that someone who had a good idea and was prepared to work hard could create one of the first programs of a particular type, getting a head start on an entire area of programming. Will Wright, for instance, bought the Commodore 64 computer as soon as it came out, shut himself in his room, and wrote what would be the first game for that computer.

Things have changed. Now there are many thousands of software companies producing programs for PCs. But that doesn't mean there isn't room for an individual programmer to set up business. The key today is to come up with an idea for a program that hasn't been written or to make dramatic improvements in a program that already exists. With more people using computers, there's plenty of room for all sorts of programs. For example, when only a small number of people had computers, there wasn't much of a market for a program that would help people keep records about their bodybuilding workouts. These days, however, there are several bodybuilding programs on the market. Is there a market for software to help people keep records of the dog shows they attend? For software that provides information for amateur sailors, such as tide tables and sunset times? For programs that help hobbyists with building and launching their model rockets? Maybe. Maybe not. The secret to a successful software entrepreneurship is to find a niche that nobody else has discovered and write a program that people will want to buy.

Good programming skills are, of course, essential to success in the software business. But as an entrepreneur, strong busi-

ness and communication skills are just as important. You can write the best program in the world, but if you don't know how to promote it, you'll never sell it.

Many entrepreneurs begin distributing their software as shareware; they give away the programs on the Internet and online services. If users like the software, they can register to get a manual, a more advanced version of the program, free upgrades, and so on. Shareware provides a way for a talented programmer to get into business with almost no initial cost—beyond the time it takes to develop the program, of course.

 # TRY IT OUT

GET THE IDEA HABIT

Every brilliant innovation starts with a single idea. Make sure you are ready to capture your best thoughts by keeping an idea notebook. Every time you have an idea about a new twist on a computer program, jot it down. Don't worry if at first you don't come up with ideas. Once you've "programmed" your mind to look for ideas, it will discover them even when you're not consciously looking for them. Keep the notebook handy because you never know when the best ideas might hit—while cleaning up in the kitchen, traveling on the school bus, or watching a movie.

Consider ways to link computer programs with specific jobs, hobbies, or tasks. Think about how programs are used: They store information, make calculations, "create" things (pictures, sounds, words), and so on. Look for ideas in which these basic procedures can be applied in some new way.

DATABASE DISCOVERY

A very quick way to get into the software business is by creating a specialized database program, a program used to store information for a particular purpose. In fact, many programs have as their primary purpose the storage of data. For instance, e-mail programs and computer phone books are basically database programs used to store e-mail messages and information about people.

Your school or home computer probably comes equipped with programs that you can use to start learning about building a database—Microsoft Works or Microsoft Excel, for instance.

After you've gotten familiar with those, create your own database. Make it useful and fun. Perhaps you could design something to keep track of homework assignments or the school's sports statistics.

✔ CHECK IT OUT

🖱 ON THE WEB

FREE FOR THE TAKING

Spend some time looking at the thousands of shareware programs available. The great thing about shareware is that you can download these programs and use them to get an idea about what other people are doing. Then you need to pay a registration fee only if you decide to continue using the program.

You can also find free shareware just for kids at some of these Web sites:

- 💡 Freeware for Kids at http://www.brothersoft.com/games/kids
- 💡 Google Shareware for Kids at http://groups.google.com/group/alt.comp.shareware.for-kids
- 💡 Kids Domain at http://www.kidsdomain.com/down
- 💡 Cybersleuth Kids at http://cybersleuth-kids.com/sleuth/Computer/Shareware/Kids/index1.htm
- 💡 Tucows Kids at http://www.tucows.com/downloads/Windows/HomeEducation/EducationReference

YOUNG ENTREPRENEURS ONLINE

Link to resources for budding businesspeople at these Web sites:

- 💡 Entrepreneur Kids at http://www.entrepreneurkids.org

- Hot Shot Business at http://www.disney.go.com/ hotshot/hsb.html
- Independent Means at http://www.independentmeans. com
- Teaching Kids Business at http://www. teachingkidsbusiness.com
- Young Biz at http://www.kidsway.com
- Youth Venture at http://www.youthventure.org

AT THE LIBRARY

ONLINE INSPIRATION

Find ideas and inspirations in these stories of famous computer pioneers and entrepreneurs:

Brackett, Virginia. *Steve Jobs: Computer Genius of Apple.* Berkeley Heights, N.J.: Enslow, 2003.

French, Laura. *Internet Pioneers: The Cyber Elite.* Berkeley Heights, N.J.: Enslow, 2002.

Marshall, David. *Bill Gates: Billionaire Computer Whiz.* Farmington Hills, Mich.: Blackbirch Press, 2003.

Morales, Leslie. *Esther Dyson: Internet Visionary.* Berkeley Heights, N.J.: Enslow, 2003.

Parks, Peggy J. *Jeff Bezos: Giants of American Industry.* Farmington Hills, Mich.: Blackbirch Press, 2005.

Peters, Craig. *Larry Ellison: Database Genius of Oracle.* Berkeley Heights, N.J.: Enslow, 2003.

———. *Steve Case: Internet Genius of America Online.* Berkeley Heights, N.J.: Enslow, 2003.

Raatma, Lucia. *Bill Gates: Computer Programmer and Entrepreneur.* New York: Ferguson, 2000.

IN THE COMPUTER BUSINESS

A successful software entrepreneur is half computer whiz and half businessperson. Catch the entrepreneurship bug with some of the ideas and activities found in the following books.

Adams, T.R. *How to be a Teenage Millionaire.* Irvine, Calif.: Entrepreneur Press, 2000.

Berg, Adriane. *The Totally Awesome Business Book for Kids.* New York: Newmarket Press, 2002.

Erlbach, Arlene. *The Kids' Business Book.* Minneapolis: Lerner, 1998.

Linecker, Adelia Cellini. *What Color Is Your Piggybank: Entrepreneurial Ideas for Self-Starting Kids.* Montreal: Lobster Press, 2004.

Mariotti, Steve. *The Young Entrepreneurs Guide to Starting and Running a Business.* New York: Three Rivers Press, 2000.

 WITH THE EXPERTS

Association of Shareware
  Professionals
PO Box 1522
Martinsville, IN 46151
http://www.asp-shareware.org

Software and Information
  Industry Association
1090 Vermont Avenue, NW,
  Sixth Floor
Washington, DC 20005
http://www.spa.org

GET ACQUAINTED

Gary Kiliany,
Software Entrepreneur

CAREER PATH

CHILDHOOD ASPIRATION: To be a scientist.

FIRST JOB: Mowing lawns and landscaping jobs.

CURRENT JOB: President of IKnowThat.com.

Gary Kiliany has been a software entrepreneur from the day he graduated from Carnegie Mellon University with a degree in electrical engineering. The goal of the company he started in 1983, Sentient Systems Technologies, was to develop electronic devices that brought the "gift of communication" to people who were unable to talk because of conditions such as cerebral palsy, autism, and traumatic brain injury.

The company eventually developed an impressive array of products that included the EyeTyper, a tool that allowed individuals to "talk" using eye-gaze techniques. The company also developed various touch-screen products that helped people communicate with others and perform routine tasks such as turning lights on and off. Sentient Systems was so successful that it was eventually bought out by another company and is now called DynaVox Technologies (http://www.dynavoxsys.com).

ALONG THE WAY

As Kiliany was building his first company, he married, had children, and became interested in how children are educated. Knowing as much as he did about the Internet and electronics, he became convinced that the power of technology could be harnessed to make learning more fun. With ideas about how he could link education and technology and start-up funding from investors, Kiliany started a second company called IKnowThat.com in 1999. Kiliany says that the goal of the company is to help children discover the magic of learning.

To achieve this, his company creates exciting games and activities that let kids—from preschoolers all the way up to sixth graders—explore learning about math, science, social studies, and language arts. The results, as you can discover for yourself at http://www.iknowthat.com, are pretty spectacular.

DOUBLE WHAMMY BUSINESS SUCCESS

Once again Kiliany has managed to create a business that both makes money and does good for other people. On the

business side of things, the company makes money in three ways. One is that they sell advertisements to pay for the free Web site. The company also sells annual subscriptions that allow families and schools to access a super-duper, deluxe section of the Web site. In addition, the company teams up with other partners such as the Discovery Learning Connection to "license their content" for use in other ways.

In the interest of doing good, Kiliany hopes that the Web site helps expose millions of children to a new way of learning—one that lets them explore their personal abilities and discover their own passions. He says this blending of abilities and passions that can some day lead children to the kind of success he enjoys in his own work.

IN A WORD

Kiliany hopes that companies like his are paving the way for a whole new kind of educational experience that loosens things up a bit. He says that today's learners need more freedom to explore so that they are better prepared to succeed in the Information Age.

As for kids who hope someday to start a company like Kiliany's, he suggests:

- ☼ Read as much as you can about computers.
- ☼ Take advantage of opportunities to write software programs (he suggests the Lego Mindstorms product as a good place to start—see http://www.mindstorms.lego.com).
- ☼ Start taking computer programming classes in middle and high school.
- ☼ Take notice of the business world by keeping up with the business section of your local newspaper.
- ☼ Most important of all, expose yourself to lots of different interests to find out what excites you most.

Kiliany urges you to use that passion to propel yourself toward a profession where you can enjoy finding success.

Systems Analyst

SHORTCUTS

GO online to learn about computers inside and out at http://www.kidsdomain.com/brain/computer/lesson.html.

READ about hot careers in technology at Get Tech at http://www.gettech.org.

TRY working your way through the math, science, and engineering activities at http://www.iknowthat.com.

WHAT IS A SYSTEMS ANALYST?

A personal computer usually sits on a desktop—or perhaps on the floor with the monitor on the desk. It's a relatively simple machine, designed for use by one person at a time. Now imagine a huge computer system, one made up of several big computers connected together, perhaps housed in a special room and used by hundreds of people, perhaps even thousands, at the same time. These systems are called mainframes.

Many large companies have such systems, and the person in charge of keeping it all going is the systems analyst. Actually, a system like this may require a team of system analysts to keep it running. These people are responsible for a variety of tasks.

Sometimes their work begins even before a computer system arrives at the company's offices. It's their job, for instance, to design the system that the company needs. They have to figure out how the computer system will be used and pick exactly the right system for the job. This is not as easy as it may sound. Go back to the single PC. It's fairly simple to decide what to get in an individual computer—the amount of memory, the type of screen, whether you want a modem or sound card, and so on. When it comes to the giant

corporate computer system, things get quite a bit trickier. It takes someone with an extremely wide range of knowledge in areas such as software, hardware, programming, and networking to make the right choices.

Once the computer system arrives, it's the systems analyst's job to get it running and make sure it stays running. That's no easy task, either. In the personal computing world, when you want to use a new program, you simply install it and start using it. But installing software on mainframes can be a huge task. In some cases, it can take weeks of programming to get the software properly configured.

In a way, a systems analyst is the middleman—someone whose job it is to figure out the best way to use technology in ways that help people, or end users, conduct business. They are essentially problem-solvers, trouble-shooters, and, in a sense, high-tech puzzle masters. They put all the pieces together—technology, software, business goals, people power—to create systems that get the job done in the most efficient and effective manner possible.

While the work obviously requires high-level computer knowledge and logical thinking skills, it also requires surprising amounts of creativity. Out-of-the-box thinkers with an ability to size up situations and make decisions thrive in this kind of work. Systems analysts require self-motivation and a certain willingness to hang in there when the going gets tough and the computer challenges get tricky.

To enter this line of work, certainly a college-level computer science program is very useful. The ability to program in languages such as Assembly, FORTRAN, COBOL, and PL/I helps as well, as they are used by these large systems. A systems analyst often starts as a personal-computer network systems administrator.

This is not the sort of job you go into directly from school. Rather, it takes plenty of experience; people tend to work their way into this job gradually. But for computer experts who think that bigger is better, this is a field to consider!

☞ TRY IT OUT

HOT ON THE COMPUTER TRAIL

Given that this is the 21st century and that computers are everywhere these days, there is a pretty good chance that you have to look no further than your own school to find a computer system. Ask the computer teacher to help you figure out how it works. Find out how many computers the school has, where they are, and how they are connected. Make a diagram or chart that illustrates how the system works.

THE PROBLEM SOLVER IS IN

Without problems to solve, a systems analyst is out of business. Get ready to tackle tomorrow's complex computer problems by learning how to tackle simple problems today. First, think about a problem that's been bugging you, your parents, or your teacher. Maybe it has something to do with a messy room, a lousy attitude, or missing homework assignments. This step is called identifying the problem, and you'll want to write down a brief description on a piece of paper. Next, make a list of all the ways you might go about fixing the problem. This is called analyzing the situation.

Finally, pick what sounds like the best solution and give it a try. This is a testing phase and may involve trying more than one solution to find out what works best. When you perform all these steps and the problem goes away, that's called problem solving.

✔ CHECK IT OUT

🖱 ON THE WEB
CYBER PUZZLES

Go online and analyze how to complete some of the puzzles found at:

- 💡 Bits and Pieces at http://www.bitsandpieces.com/arcade.aspx
- 💡 Jigsaw Puzzles Online at http://www.thekidzpage.com/onlinejigsawpuzzles
- 💡 Learning Planet Puzzles at http://www.learningplanet.com/act/puzzles.asp
- 💡 Puzzability at http://www.puzzability.com/puzzles/index.shtml
- 💡 Puzzler at http://www.actualentertainment.com/puzzle.htm
- 💡 Super Kids Logic at http://www.superkids.com/aweb/tools/logic

📚 AT THE LIBRARY

COMPUTER LITERACY

The following books will help you get better acquainted with the number-one tool of the systems analyst's job—computers.

Bridgeman, Roger. *Eyewitness: Technology.* New York: DK Publishing, 2000.

Cassedy, Patrice. *Computer Technology.* Farmington Hills, Mich.: Lucent Books, 2004.

Ladd, Kimberly. *Bytes of Bits: Getting Started in Computer Science.* Philadelphia: Xlibris, 2003.

Parker, Steve. *Computers Now and Into the Future.* North Mankato, Minn.: Thameside Press, 2003.

Rooney, Anne. *Computers: The Cutting Edge.* Portsmouth, N.H.: Heinemann, 2005.

Sommervill, Barbara. *The History of Computers.* Chanhassen, Minn.: Child's World, 2006.

LOGICAL WHODUNITS

There's nothing quite like a little mystery and mayhem to sharpen the logical-thinking skills you'll need as a systems analyst. You'll find plenty of both in books such as:

Cameron, Vicki. *Clue Mysteries: 15 Whodunits to Solve in Minutes.* Philadelphia: Running Press, 2003.

———. *More Clue Mysteries: 15 More Whodunits to Solve in Minutes.* Philadelphia: Running Press, 2003.

Sukach, Jim. *Wicked Whodunits: Dr. Quicksilver Mini Mysteries.* New York: Sterling, 2005.

Weber, Jim. *Absolutely Amazing Five Minute Mysteries.* Philadelphia: Running Press, 2004.

———. *Utterly Ingenious Five Minute Mysteries.* Philadelphia: Running Press, 2004.

🗣< WITH THE EXPERTS

Association of Information Technology Professionals
401 North Michigan Avenue, Suite 2400
Chicago, IL 60611
http://www.aitp.org

Institute for Certification of Computing Professionals
2350 East Devon Avenue, Suite 115
Des Plaines, IL 60018-4610
http://www.iccp.org

Institute of Electrical and Electronics Engineers
3 Park Avenue, 17th Floor
New York, NY 10016
http://www.ieee.org

GET ACQUAINTED

Rob Kolstad, Systems Analyst

CAREER PATH

CHILDHOOD ASPIRATION: To be a TV repairman so he could work with electronics and watch TV all day!

FIRST JOB: Selling soft drinks and seat cushions at University of Oklahoma football games.

CURRENT POSITION: Executive Director of SAGE, a professional organization for systems administrators.

You wouldn't be wrong if you said that computers came naturally to Rob Kolstad. Back in the mid-1960s when he was in middle school, his first notion of computers was of putting special cards into a big machine (computers were huge back then!) so that information would come out. One day he happened upon a teacher puzzling over some pages with lots of numbers on them. The pages turned out to be a computer program the teacher was trying to write. When Kolstad took one look at the code and offered what turned out to be rather brilliant advice, the teacher informed him that he had a "knack for computers."

Several decades and a wildly successful career later, it turns out that the teacher was absolutely right.

COMPUTER PIONEER

When it came time to go to college, Kolstad attended Southern Methodist University, in Dallas, one of the first colleges in the nation to offer a computer science degree. He followed that up with a degree in electrical engineering from Notre Dame and a doctorate in software from the University of Illinois. With all that knowledge under his belt, he officially launched his computer career with a company called Convex which was involved in developing supercomputers that sold for about $1 million each.

It didn't take long for Kolstad to earn a reputation that has held true throughout his career: He was the guy to call when you wanted to make computer problems go away. The main thrust of his entire career can be summed up in three words—make things work. With that deceptively simple mandate, he worked his way around the world in corporations large and small. He recalls one time being flown out to help a client in France whose computer network wouldn't work. Within a couple hours, he had determined the solution and was on to help other clients in the area.

Another time he was working for a company specializing in security conferences and his boss came to him with what would be a nightmare of a problem for anyone. His e-mail box was back-logged with 17,000 e-mails, and he didn't know how to handle all of them. So Kolstad hammered out a software program that sifted through the email, got rid of the useless stuff, and processed e-mail every couple hours.

Kolstad says that his software program saved the company lots of money because a computer was able to do what it would have taken several people lots of boring hours to do. Once he got the software right, the computer did the job for free.

HAVE COMPUTER, WILL TRAVEL

Nowadays, Kolstad travels the world speaking at conferences, teaching courses, and hosting computer game shows. He also continues in one of his favorite roles—USA Computer Olympiad head coach. He was actually one of the original coaches for this premier international computer contest for high school students. The USACO is a nonprofit group that works with more than 33,000 students in over 90 nations. Kolstad invites you to check out their Web site at http://www.usaco.org and make plans to get involved when you get a little older.

MAKE IT WORK

Kolstad offers two bits of advice to anyone wanting to enjoy their career—no matter what it involves. First, he says to find your passion, a challenge that isn't always as easy for others as it was for him with his instant connection with computers. He says that if someone says they want to be a brain surgeon but spends all his or her spare time playing sports, he or she may want to think again about what really turns them on. Second, once someone identifies their passion, he or she needs to find ways to pursue it as a part of their career or life. In short, Kolstad says to find it and do it!

Systems Manager

WHAT IS A SYSTEMS MANAGER?

Running a major computer system is almost like running a military operation. There are other people involved, and the systems manager has to make sure that everything comes together in the right way at the right time. He or she is responsible for the overall management of the system. The systems manager may not actually work directly with computers but is in charge of all the people who do. You could say that the systems manager is the computer boss.

In today's technological age, this job has become even more important. Using technology in the smartest way possible often means the difference between great success and ho-hum survival. A good systems manager can give a company the edge it needs to stay competitive by staying on top of everything from making the company's technology plan and keeping the company's network safe from hackers and other risks to providing a stable online environment that allows the company to conduct business online.

Planning, coordinating, directing, researching, and designing are words that describe much of the work performed by systems managers. They also manage the work of systems analysts, computer programmers, support specialists, and other types of computer-related professionals. Making sure

that these people keep the company's systems humming along with the best hardware and most recent versions of software is one task often found on the system manager's to-do list. Keeping the information-technology team working to develop effective computer networks, create Internet and intranet sites, and coordinate special programming efforts are other responsibilities.

When something goes wrong with the system, the systems manager is the one most likely to be held responsible, which is why this type of work generally requires quite a bit of experience. Systems managers typically start off as programmers or systems analysts.

Systems manager is a catch-all title that describes the basic function of this job. In some companies this position includes additional duties and is called the chief technology officer (CTO). This person is in charge of everything and anything to do with the company's technology in much the same way that a chief executive officer (or CEO) is in charge of the company's business operations. In other companies, the position is called management information systems (MIS)

director. In a similar but more focused vein, project managers are responsible for managing everything related to specific technology projects.

If this is the sort of job you might aspire to, start by gaining the technical knowledge you need. A computer science degree, coupled with experience in programming or computer networking, can be a great start. You'll eventually have to get some business training and experience as well. Many people take business courses in the evenings, working to earn a master's degree in business administration (MBA) while working full time.

TRY IT OUT

THE FAMILY THAT COMPUTES TOGETHER

Appoint yourself the family information systems manager. Your first job is to find out how each family member has been affected by technology in the past. Start with the oldest family member—grandparents are good, great-grandparents are even better. Ask them about the new technologies that developed as they were growing up. You may be surprised to discover the kinds of technologies—television, for example—that didn't even exist back then. Then find out about their favorite ways to use technology now. Ask them what they wish someone would invent to make life easier for them. Compile their answers in one column of a chart with separate sections for past, present, and future.

Repeat this process with the next oldest—either parents or grandparents. Then do it again until it's your turn. When you are finished, you'll have a high-tech version of your family tree—and a good idea of the kind of assessment process systems mangers use in their work.

CYBER SHOPPING

Systems managers often wrestle with the desire to have the latest and greatest technology and the need to stick within

their company's technology budget. This means they need to shop around to find the best deals on the best equipment. Just suppose your teacher announces that your class just received funding to purchase 25 laptop computers—one for each student. Wouldn't that be awesome? The system needs to include a high-resolution color screen, wireless Internet capabilities, and enough memory to store lots of homework assignments (ugh!). Your job is to go online to Web sites for three of the major computer manufacturers and find the best deal possible.

- ☼ Apple at http://www.apple.com
- ☼ Dell at http://www.dell.com
- ☼ Gateway at http://www.gateway.com

Make a chart to compare features and prices for their most expensive and least expensive models.

 # CHECK IT OUT

ON THE WEB

WHAT'S NEXT?

Technology has come a long way in the past 100 years and in just the past 10 years as well. Systems managers have to stay one step ahead of all the progress in order to do their jobs well. Following are some Web sites where you can find out more about where technology has been and where it's headed.

- ☼ Adventures in Science at http://www.collections. ic.gc.ca/science
- ☼ Discovery Channel Tech Guide at http://dsc.discovery. com/guides/tech/tech.html
- ☼ How Stuff Works Express at http://express. howstuffworks.com
- ☼ Intel Museum at http://www.intel.com/museum

⚗ *Popular Science* at http://www.popsci.com/popsci
⚗ The Technology Museum of Innovation at http://www.thetech.org

INNOVATION IN PRINT
Find ideas and inspiration in the following books:

DK Publishing. *Eyewonder: Invention* (DK Eyewitness Books). New York: DK Publishing, 2005.

Halstead, Rachel. *Technology: Hands on History.* London, England: Southwater, 2004.

———. *Technology: Hands on Science.* London, England: Southwater, 2004.

Packard, Mary. *High Tech Inventions: True Tales.* Danbury, Conn.: Children's Press, 2004.

Steward, David. *Brainpower: What's the Big Idea?* Hauppauge, N.Y.: Baroons, 2005.

St. George, Judith, and David Small. *So You Want to be An Inventor?* New York: Puffin Books, 2005.

Williams, Marcia. *Hurray for Inventors!* Cambridge, Mass.: Candlewick Press, 2005.

Wood, Richard. *Great Inventions.* New York: Barnes and Noble, 2003.

Woodford, Chris. *Cool Stuff and How It Works.* New York: DK Publishing, 2005.

🗣⚒ WITH THE EXPERTS

Association for Computer Operations Managers
742 East Chapman Avenue
Orange, CA 92866
http://www.afcom.com

Association for Computing Machinery
1515 Broadway
New York, NY 10036
http://www.acm.org/

GET ACQUAINTED

Timothy Vann,
Systems Manager

CAREER PATH

CHILDHOOD ASPIRATION: To work with electronic equipment.

FIRST JOB: Cleaning wire out of farm equipment in the Kansas heat.

CURRENT JOB: Field operations manager at cellular phone compnay.

A LITTLE DETOUR ALONG THE WAY

Having been raised on a farm, Timothy Vann was always fascinated with equipment of all kinds, particularly electronic devices. He was the one his siblings would look for when something needed to be fixed. He came to his current career after trying out several ventures.

Vann left home after high school and attended a junior college. His education was cut short by a serious car accident that required a steel plate being placed in his leg (he still has problems getting through security at airports) and a long recovery period. Upon his recuperation (and marriage to a young woman back home), he began in earnest the pursuit of his career.

From his hometown to Phoenix, Phoenix to Kansas City, Kansas City to Denver, Denver to Oklahoma City, and back to Denver, Vann was in pursuit of his dream job. Along the way, he attended technical schools and built storage sheds to pay for his education. After scrimping and saving, he finished an accelerated course at a technical institute and graduated with an associate's degree in 18 months.

THE PURSUIT CONTINUES

The cellular phone industry was in its infancy when, through a stroke of luck and the help of a mentor, Vann obtained a job with a new cellular phone company as a "drive test person." Many miles were put on his vehicle as he drove around the state, collecting data to plot coverage maps and dealing with interference issues. He then was promoted to an information systems technician, installing phone systems and data system work stations.

MORE EXCITEMENT TO COME

Through hard work, long hours, and perseverance, Vann was promoted to systems technician, working on equipment in the field. From this he advanced to senior systems technician and is now the field operations manager. He has a cellular phone with him at all times as he supervises and manages people who do the day-to-day repair and maintenance on the hundreds of cellular sites across his statewide territory in Colorado.

SQUIRREL CATASTROPHES

Every day brings new challenges. There are no "typical" days for Vann. There are always glitches of one kind or another—software glitches that cause hardware failures, for instance. And, an occasional squirrel chewing on coaxial cables can knock out service in an entire city!

Technical Support Representative

WHAT IS A TECHNICAL SUPPORT REPRESENTATIVE?

Technical support representatives—also known as help desk techs—are computer experts who answer questions about computer programs or computer hardware. If you've spent much time working with computers, you may have already discovered that it is a good idea to have help available around the clock. (For some strange reason, computers never seem to crash during business hours!)

There are two types of businesses in which teams of technical support representatives work. One place is at companies that produce or publish specific types of computer software or hardware. For instance, if a program you are working in starts doing weird things, you can call the company that produces it and ask them what to do to fix it. Or, if you are trying to install a new modem in your computer, you could call the company that makes the modem and ask how to make it work. While the techs that work in places like these must have a good overall understanding of computers, they must be whizzes at working with the specific product they represent.

Another place you are likely to find technical support representatives is at any good-size company that uses computers. The people working at these companies depend on their in-house techs to bail them out of all sorts of computer problems, so you can imagine that they have to know their way around quite an assortment of equipment and applications.

Of course, having someone sitting by the phone waiting for customers to call is a very expensive way to fix problems, so most companies regard it as a last resort—or even charge customers who consult the technical support department. Instead, many companies now take care of the most common problems with recorded messages detailing how to fix them. Many companies also have documents that can be faxed to their customers.

But the telephone is not the only tool used to help customers fix their problems. These days many companies are also using e-mail, Web sites, and Internet or online service discussion groups as ways to get information to their customers.

How does all this innovation affect technical

support representatives? Not so long ago, the tech simply provided help over the telephone line. That's still an important part of the job, but now so is answering e-mail, writing documents to be placed at a Web site or to be added to the fax-on-demand system, and answering questions in Internet discussion groups or chat rooms. Small companies in particular also use technical support staff to test new products, since they are so in tune with how consumers might use them.

You don't need a degree to get into this business. Employers are looking for people who enjoy working with computers and who have a wide range of knowledge about different software and hardware systems; in short, they want people who are comfortable around computers. Communication skills are important, too. It's one thing to be a computer expert and quite another to be able to communicate your knowledge in a way that a typical computer user can understand. Strong verbal and written skills are a must for this type of work.

The job involves equal parts of working with computers and helping people. It helps if you enjoy both and are eager to keep learning new things. Technology changes rapidly, and you'll have to stay a step ahead of it to offer the best support to your customers.

 TRY IT OUT

TECH FOR HIRE

Isn't it a great feeling to be able to do something that the adults around you can't do? It seems that your generation has the edge on all this technology. Many adults are computer illiterate, barely able to turn on the computer, much less do something useful with it.

That's where you come in. Find one of these adults and volunteer to teach him or her the basics. Your potential "customers" might include a parent or grandparent, a neighbor, or even a teacher.

You might explain how to open programs and files in Microsoft Windows or how to work with a word processor. You'll find that things you think are obvious are not clear to someone who has no experience with computers, so think carefully about how you explain things. Be as clear as possible, and avoid using computer jargon whenever possible. At the end of each session, give your student a "report card" praising his or her progress and making suggestions for homework.

COMPUTER TUTOR

Chances are pretty good that your school has a computer lab. Ask your computer teacher if they'd like some help working with students who are having trouble catching on. You might find time to do so during the school day or set up regular hours before or after school. You'll learn a lot about computers and get some great experience to add to your résumé. You may also want to consider getting involved in any programs your school offers for peer tutoring. These programs usually involve a student who is especially good in one subject helping another student who is struggling with the same subject in some way. Other programs involve having older students work with younger students. Still other "buddy" types of programs pair up an older student with a younger one for a special reading time. Wherever or however you do it, the goal is to get some practice teaching other people how to do something.

✔ CHECK IT OUT

🖱 ON THE WEB

TECH SUPPORT ONLINE

See how tech support is done by visiting some of these online tech support Web sites—some just for kids, others for all types of computer users:

- ☀ Ask Me Help Desk at http://www.askmehelpdesk.com
- ☀ C/Net Help.com at http://reviews.cnet.com/ 4002-7600_7-5082858.html

- Kids Compute at http://www.kidcompute.com
- Kids Online Resources at http://www.kidsolr.com/technicalsupport
- Microsoft Product Solution Center at http://support.microsoft.com/select/?target=hub
- Zoom Tech Support By Kids For Kids at http://pbskids.org/zoom/help/technical

CYBER COMPUTER SCHOOL

Besides online tech support, another way to teach people how to use computers and various software programs is to provide online tutorials. It's like using a computer to teach a class. Following are some links to see how it's done:

- Cybersleuth Kids at http://cybersleuth-kids.com/sleuth/Computer/Tutorials
- EX-Tutor for Using Computers http://www.elmlane.com/ez_tutor/index.html
- Microsoft Student Home Page at http://www.microsoft.com/education/collegestudents.mspx
- Technology Tutorials Found on the Web at http://www.internet4classrooms.com/on-line2.htm
- Tutorials for Kids, Parents, Teachers at http://www.iage.com/tutorial.html#Kids

 ## AT THE LIBRARY

MINDING YOUR PS AND QS

Technical support representatives are often the first (and sometimes only) human contact that customers have with a company, so it's really important that they make a good impression. The following books provide tips on minding your manners, communicating effectively, managing your time, and handling the ups and downs that come with dealing with the public like a pro.

Elizabeth, Mary. *Painless Speaking.* Hauppauge, N.Y.: Barrons, 2003.

Espeland, Pamela and Elizabeth Verdick. *Smart Ways to Spend Your Time.* Minneapolis: Free Spirit, 2005.

Ferguson. *Communication Skills: Career Skills Library.* New York: Ferguson, 2004.

——. *Organizing Skills: Career Skills Library.* New York: Ferguson, 2004.

Kennedy, Michelle. *Manners: Last Straw Strategies.* Hauppauge, N.Y.: Barrons, 2004.

Otfinoski, Stephen. *Speaking Up, Speaking Out.* Minneapolis: Millbrook Press, 1997.

Parker, Alex. *How Rude! The Teenagers Guide to Good Manners, Proper Behavior, and Not Grossing People Out.* Minneapolis: Free Spirit, 2005.

Schwartz, Linda. *What Would You Do: A Kid's Guide to Sticky Situations.* Owings Mills, Md.: Learning Works, 2003.

WITH THE EXPERTS

Association of Personal Computer User Groups
3155 East Patrick Lane, Suite 1
Las Vegas, NV 89120
http://www.apcug.net

Association of Support Professionals Association
122 Barnard Avenue
Watertown, MA 02472
http://www.asponline.com

Software Support Professionals Association
11031 Via Frontera, Suite A
San Diego, CA 92127
http://www.thesspa.com

GET ACQUAINTED

Elias AbuGhazaleh, Technical
Support Representative

CAREER PATH

CHILDHOOD ASPIRATION: To do anything with computers.

FIRST JOB: Answering the technical support phone line at NovaStor.

CURRENT JOB: Senior manager, software quality assurance at an international software development company.

LOVE AT FIRST BYTE

Elias AbuGhazaleh decided that he wanted to work with computers when he was 12, when he first used an Apple personal computer. He wasn't quite sure what he wanted to do, but he knew it had to be something involving computers. "I used to hack programs in the evenings after school and learned a lot of different programs and systems," he says. By the time he reached high school, he realized—or at least thought he realized—that he wanted to be a computer programmer.

Things didn't quite turn out the way he expected, though. He went to the California Lutheran University to earn a computer science degree, intending to become a programmer when he graduated. During his senior year, he took a part-time job with NovaStor Corporation, answering their technical support calls. NovaStor sells backup, encryption, and anti-virus software, and it was AbuGhazaleh's job to help NovaStor's clients figure out how to fix any problems they might have with these programs.

WHAT NEXT?

After graduating, AbuGhazaleh took a full-time position with NovaStor, working in technical support but hoping to move into a programming position when one became available. But that programming position never did become available. Instead, NovaStor promoted him to manager of the technical support department and added another responsibility: managing the company's quality assurance department. That's the department that tests the company's products and ensures that they are working correctly. AbuGhazaleh believes that these two functions—technical support and quality assurance—should always be linked, although in large companies they're generally two very separate departments. Ideally, however, people who sit and talk with customers all day, learning about problems with the products, should also be involved with testing products and recommending changes to those products. After all, these people know what customers want and what customers find frustrating about the company's products. AbuGhazaleh rotates staff between the two departments, letting his seven technical support people help test and recommend changes to products and making his quality assurance people spend time talking to customers on the technical support line.

TECHNICAL CAREER TRACK

Working with NovaStor got AbuGhazaleh's career off to a great start. He enjoyed starting out with a smaller company where he was given the opportunity to learn about different aspects of the business and try out different levels of responsibility. He especially enjoyed the technical, hands-on aspects of the work. When he was promoted to management, he was pleasantly surprised to discover how much he liked it.

In fact, AbuGhazaleh liked management so well that he eventually accepted a senior management position with a huge international software development company—even though the new job required a move all the way from California to Florida. Now he works for a company that employs more than 16,000 people worldwide. His job involves managing a large group of quality assurance software testers and allows him to apply a blend of technical expertise and people skills every day.

THE REAL PICTURE

AbuGhazaleh is happy to be where he is now. The computer industry is an exciting one. It's the future: "Computers are everywhere. Everything involves computers these days; I can't imagine why anyone wouldn't want to be involved in this business."

AbuGhazaleh has a degree in computer science, but he recognizes that kids can get into the technical support business without one. "Fool around with computers," he says. "You need to be up to date with the computer industry, have a wide range of knowledge, understand all the jargon, and be capable of talking with people intelligently."

It also doesn't hurt to be well versed in one or more programming languages such as Java or C++. His best advice is to take time to learn and study and be ready to grow with the industry.

Technical Writer

SHORTCUTS

GO visit the Society for Technical Communication's Web site (http://stc.org).

READ *The Elements of Style* by William Strunk and E. B. White (New York: Allyn & Bacon, 1999). It will help you learn to write clearly and concisely.

TRY writing some instructions for a product you use, perhaps a product that came with terrible documentation.

SKILL SET

✔ COMPUTERS

✔ WRITING

✔ SCIENCE

WHAT IS A TECHNICAL WRITER?

Have you ever tried to use a computer program's user manual and thought you could describe how to use the program better? Well, maybe you should consider a career in technical writing. A technical writer can do any number of things: write user manuals for computer programs, instructions for using complicated telecommunications equipment, and information that will be published on a Web site. Technical writers write about all sorts of products and processes, which is one of the nice things about this career: There's a lot of variety.

Technical writers explain how to use things or do things, and as the items we use every day seem to be getting more complicated, there's a lot of explaining to do. For every computer, computer program, telephone, answering machine, printer, scanner, fax machine, car, motorbike, watch, calculator, or whatever else you can imagine, instructions have to be written. Instructions are also required for many toys, bicycles, and games. The instructions produced by technical writers may fit on a single piece of paper, or they may take up thousands of pages in several volumes of loose-leaf binders.

Technical writing is the sort of job that tends to expand. Your employer may need someone to write some promotional materials—brochures or flyers, for instance. If the company doesn't have a public relations or advertising writer (and most don't), you may be asked to step in and create these things. Writers often work on Web sites too; in fact, many webmasters start off as technical writers.

Technical writers often write proposals, special documents used by companies when looking to start a new venture. A proposal describes what the company will do for a client, often in great detail. Technical writers sometimes write magazine articles designed to promote their companies, and some write the computer books you see for sale in your local bookstore.

A good technical writer must be able to write well. But just as important is the ability to structure the flow of information. You may be able to write the most beautiful prose, but unless you can explain things in a clear and logical manner, you won't be good technical writer. You must be able to learn quickly too. If you find it difficult to pick up new ideas and learn how to use new products, this probably isn't the career for you. But if you really enjoy the challenge of learning new things, you'll feel at home with technical writing.

This is a booming business, with the demand for technical writers growing rapidly. Consequently, it's fairly well paid, and there are lots of opportunities for freelancers. If at some point in your career you decide you want to work for yourself, you may be

able to build a successful freelance technical writing business, as many others have done.

Most technical writers do not have technical writing degrees; such degrees are relatively new, and most of the more senior writers just fell into technical writing, almost by accident. Many journalists become technical writers (because it's much better paid), as do geologists, biologists, programmers, and people with business or English degrees—just about anyone. Still, if you're interested in this career, you should think about getting a technical writing degree. A computer science degree would also be useful and would provide you with more flexibility in your career choice later. There are also a number of correspondence courses on technical writing, which could be combined with courses in computer science.

 TRY IT OUT

WRITE TECH

Most technical writing comes down to this—explaining how to do something in a way other people can understand. Granted, technical writing tends to be about complicated subjects, which is why it's called *technical* writing. But you can apply the basic principles of clear, step-by-step technical writing to simple tasks such as:

- ☼ How to make a peanut butter and jelly sandwich
- ☼ How to make a bed
- ☼ How to tease a younger brother or sister without getting caught by your parents

So go ahead. See if you can write simple, straightforward instructions for tasks like these or one that you make up yourself.

THE WRITE STUFF

Writers write. It's as much a part of who they are and what they do as blinking or breathing. Try making writing a habit by

keeping a notebook or journal by your bed or on your desk at home. Take at least a few minutes every day to write down observations, ideas, interesting quotes you heard, new words you learned, reviews about books you read or movies you watched, reactions to things that happened at home or school, and anything else you can think of that gets you putting words on paper.

 CHECK IT OUT

 ON THE WEB
WRITER'S WEB

The Internet is full of great resources for young writers. Start your cybersurfing at Web sites that include:

- Creative Writing for Kids at http://www.iknowthat.com/com/L3?Area=L2_LanguageArts
- Grammar Bites at http://www.chompchomp.com
- Grammar Gorillas at http://www.funbrain.com/grammar
- I Know That at http://www.iknowthat.com/com/L3?Area=L2_LanguageArts
- Kid Authors at http://www.kidauthors.com
- KidPub at http://www.kidpub.com
- Kids on the Net at http://kotn.ntu.ac.uk
- MysteryNet at http://kids.mysterynet.com
- Word Central at http://www.wordcentral.com
- The Write Site at http://www.writesite.org
- Writing Den at http://www2.actden.com/writ_den

WORD SMART

What would a writer do without words? Make sure you never have to find out by building your own vocabulary with regular visits to these "word a day" Web sites:

- http://www.wordsmith.org/words/today.html
- http://dictionary.reference.com/wordoftheday

- http://www.nytimes.com/learning/students/wordofday
- http://www.oed.com/cgi/display/wotd
- http://www.m-w.com/cgi-bin/mwwod.pl

AT THE LIBRARY

READ TO WRITE

Behind every good writer is a good reader. And one of the best ways to prepare for a career as a writer is to read—anything, everything. Of course, another good way to prepare to become a writer is to write. The following books let you do both, since you'll be reading about writing.

Buckley, Annie, and Kathleen Coyle. *Once Upon a Time: Creative Writing for Kids.* San Francisco: Chronicle, 2004.

Gould, Judith, and Mary Burke. *Write Now! A Guide to Getting Starting.* Carthage, Ill.: Teaching and Learning, 2005.

Olin, Rebecca. *Kids Write! Fantasy, Sci Fi, Autobiography, Adventure and More.* Nashville, Tenn.: Ideals, 2006.

Rhatigan, Joe. *In Print! 40 Cool Publishing Projects for Kids.* New York: Sterling, 2004.

———. *Write Now! The Ultimate Grab a Pen, Get the Words, Have a Blast Writing Book.* Asheville, N.C.: Lark Books, 2005.

WITH THE EXPERTS

Institute of Electrical and Electronic Engineers/Professional
  Communication Society
445 Hoes Lane
Piscataway, NJ 08854
http://www.ieeepcs.org

Society for Technical Communication
901 North Stuart Street, Suite 904
Arlington, VA 22203
http://www.stc.org

Special Interest Group on Design of Communication
c/o ACM
1515 Broadway
New York, NY 10036
http://www.sigdoc.org

GET ACQUAINTED

Brenda Dickson Curry,
Technical Writer

CAREER PATH

CHILDHOOD ASPIRATION: To be a veterinarian.

FIRST JOB: Scheduling ads at a radio station.

CURRENT JOB: Freelance technical writer.

A CHANGE OF PLANS

Brenda Curry has always enjoyed writing. In elementary school she used to write poems and read them in class. But originally she wanted to be a vet because she loved animals so.

By college, she was studying business but soon found that she preferred her elective journalism courses (and got better grades in them—a great clue for knowing you're on the right track). In her sophomore year at the University of Houston, she changed her major. She graduated with a major in journalism and a minor in English, specializing in public relations and advertising.

Before graduating, however, Curry had already uncovered her talent. The Harris County Child Protective Services Department asked the students in her college advertising class to write ads encouraging people to adopt minority children. Each student wrote a piece, and everyone voted for the best one. Curry's ad won and was produced for television.

RADIO WRITING

Encouraged by the success of her first television piece, Curry decided to go into copywriting—the business of writing ads. But, she found it to be a hard business to break into, with jobs few and far between. "The mistake I made was not taking an internship while in college," she says. "It's a good way to graduate with some experience in the job you want."

So instead of going into copywriting, Curry began work at a radio station. She'd hoped for the chance to investigate and report consumer complaints but got stuck in scheduling ads instead. Frustrated with waiting for the consumer reports program, she moved on and took an editing job working for a NASA subcontractor.

This company, Computer Sciences Corporation, was creating software and related documentation for NASA mission control and the Apollo program. Curry began by editing a variety of technical books. The first was on something called a thermal vacuuming system.

WRITING AT LAST

Curry was soon promoted from editing to writing. She got a raise and her first technical writing job. She worked for NASA for about three years, and then she took a job with the Texas Agricultural Extension Service, writing a newsletter and producing workshops. That lasted about six years. Next she returned to NASA for seven years and finally moved from Houston to Dallas to be with her family.

Her first job in Dallas was working through a technical service agency at Spring, the telecommunications giant. Technical service agencies find temporary staff for companies and hire many technical writers. Contracts often last for years, although they can sometimes be canceled at very short notice. In fact, when the Spring contract was canceled after three months, Curry was devastated. She'd never imag-

ined she was leaving a long-term position with NASA for something that would last just a few weeks!

FREELANCE—A GREAT WAY TO GO

Things bounced back quickly enough, though, and Curry is glad that she decided to stick with freelance writing. She's worked almost exclusively on contract for the last ten years, working for companies such as Data General, Texas Instruments, Ericsson, Mobil, and Nortel. The work is plentiful, and it pays better than full-time technical writing positions.

As a mother, she likes the flexible hours too. She's able to attend school meetings and schedule doctor's appointments during the day and easily make up the time later.

She finds the job interesting and enjoys making the research, the writing, the page layout, and editing come together like a giant puzzle. Curry finds satisfaction in getting them all together just right.

Trainer

SHORTCUTS

GO take every opportunity you can to talk in front of your class.

READ some of the greatest speeches in history at http://www.historyplace.com/speeches/previous.htm.

TRY learning a new program or computer game and teaching your friends, step-by-step, how to work with the program.

SKILL SET

✔ TALKING
✔ COMPUTERS
✔ WRITING

WHAT IS A TRAINER?

In this world of rapidly changing computer technology, an education doesn't end when you leave high school or even college. Millions of people have had to learn completely new skills, long after they thought their education was over.

On the technology side of things, the computer trainer is responsible for teaching people new skills. Trainers are sometimes employed by large corporations. A company with thousands of employees always has someone who needs training, so such companies can afford to have a full-time training department. Smaller companies, however, use the services of computer training companies, another major employer of trainers. These companies often have their own office buildings, with several classrooms full of computers. Sometimes they do on-site training too; that is, they send trainers to a company's building and train the employees there. Some companies also market their courses directly to individuals, renting large rooms in various cities to carry out one- or two-day seminars. And many trainers start their own businesses. As with a number of careers in computing, training is an ideal freelance occupation.

A good trainer is a people person, someone who enjoys working with people all day. Many trainers have a great deal of technical experience, but they've discovered they prefer

working with people rather than with machines. Other trainers knew right from the start what they wanted to do, and
they have learned the technical knowledge they need so that
they can train others.

If you're interested in a training career, you'll have to be
comfortable talking in front of groups of people; that's what
you'll be doing most of the time, after all. A strong computing background is important too, but there's generally no
requirement to have a computer science degree in order to
get started in this career. Many trainers have no degree of
any kind. Teaching abilities are more important than technical knowledge: often, training companies will teach you what
you need to know, as long as they believe you have the skills
and personality to be a good trainer. And because there's
such a wide range of information that has to be taught,
there's room for trainers of vary-
ing backgrounds and technical
abilities. Advanced programming courses, for example,
must be taught by someone
with a strong programming

background. But courses on how to use a word processor or spreadsheet can be taught by any capable trainer, once he or she has learned the program.

You need to be outgoing, understanding, and patient. Teaching can be a difficult job, and sometimes you need the patience to allow students to absorb things (ask your teachers about this!). You also must be able to break down complicated subjects into smaller, easier-to-understand blocks. A good trainer can quickly see how a subject is made up of smaller parts, then teach those parts one by one.

Learn as much about computers as you can, and perhaps focus on one area you enjoy: graphics software, desktop-publishing software, or Web site authoring software, for instance. The more you know about computers in general, however, the more attractive you will be to employers. Having been employed in a retail computer store helps, as such work provides a good overall view of personal computing, both hardware and software, and gives you lots of contact with the public.

TRY IT OUT

A PICTURE IS WORTH A MILLION WORDS
Trainers everywhere back up their words with pictures using a variety of audiovisual materials. One especially popular tool is Microsoft PowerPoint, a multimedia software tool that you may already be familiar with. If not, you can learn the ropes (or get a good refresher course) at the PowerPoint in the Classroom online tutorial at http://www.actden.com/pp. Go through each of the lessons and use what you learn to make up a PowerPoint presentation on a subject you want to know more about.

I HAVE A DREAM TOO
One of the greatest speeches of the 20th century was undoubtedly Martin Luther King's "I Have a Dream" speech. You can find links that will let you listen to the original speech and read the full text. Pay careful attention to the way Dr. King

used words to convey important ideas, and then use the worksheet to create your own version of the speech at http://www. educationworld.com/a_lesson/02/lp248-04.shtml.

TEACH YOUNGER KIDS

Ask your computer teacher if you can help teach some of the younger kids in your school. This will offer great experience in patience! Teaching young kids can be very challenging because they often have short attention spans. Your task is to try as hard as you can to teach them how to use a program, such as a math game, a word processor, or graphics program, while accepting that they may not be listening quite as closely as you'd like.

And remember, break concepts down into little steps; then teach the steps one by one.

✔ CHECK IT OUT

🖱 ON THE WEB

NEWSWORTHY ARGUMENTS

Learning to weigh the pros and cons of various issues is a great way to hone your communication skills. And keeping up with the latest news is a surefire way to become an interesting and well-informed person. Put the two skills together by picking out a late-breaking news story found at the following Web sites.

- ☼ CNN for Students at http://www.cnnstudentnews. cnn.com
- ☼ Kids News Room at http://www.kidsnewsroom.org
- ☼ Time for Kids at http://www.timeforkids.com
- ☼ Washington Post for Kids at http://www.washingtonpost. com/wpdyn.kids.post

Make a chart comparing the good news and bad news parts of the story or arguing for or against the viewpoint presented in the story.

WALKING DICTIONARY

Trainers use words to paint pictures that help people "see" how to do new things. Knowing lots of words, or vocabulary, is one way to make sure that the verbal pictures trainers paint are masterpieces. Following are some fun Web sites and resources to help you build your own vocabulary.

- Build Your Own Dictionary at http://www.wordcentral.com/dictionarybuilders.html
- Daily Buzzword at http://www.wordcentral.com/dailybuzzword.html
- Vocabulary University at http://www.vocabulary.com

AT THE LIBRARY

WORDS FOR THE WISE

Communication is the name of the training game. Learn how to talk so others will listen, speak in public without being scared half to death, and convince people to do things your way with tips found in books that include:

Daley, Patrick. *50 Debate Tricks for Kids.* N.Y.: Instructor Books, 2001.

Douglas, Ali. *Girl Talk: Games to Get the Gab Going at Home, at School, Or Anywhere Girls Go.* Middleton, Wisc.: American Girls, 2005.

Elizabeth, Mary. *Painless Speaking.* Hauppauge, New York: Barrons, 2003.

Ferguson. *Communication Skills.* New York: Ferguson, 2004.

Rossi, Amy. *Kids Communicate.* Washington, D.C.: National Geographic, 2002.

Ryan, Margaret. *Extraordinary Oral Presentations.* Danbury, Conn.: Franklin Watts, 2005.

Just for fun, learn a few tricks from some fine feathered (and furry!) friends of the animal kingdom in:

Jenkins, Steve. *Slap, Squeak, Scatter: How Animals Communicate.* New York: Houghton, Mifflin, 2001.

Kaner, Etta. *Animal Talk: How Animals Communicate Through Sight, Sound, and Smell.* Tonawanda, N.Y.: Kids Can Press, 2002.

✍ WITH THE EXPERTS

American Society for
  Training & Development
1640 King Street, Box 1443
Alexandria, VA 22313-2043
http://www.astd.org

ITrain (International Association of
  Information Technology Trainers)
PMB 616
6030-M Marshalee Drive
Elkridge, MD 21075-5987
http://www.itrain.org

GET ACQUAINTED

Molly Roberts, Trainer

CAREER PATH

CHILDHOOD ASPIRATION:
To be president of the United States or a doctor.

FIRST JOB: Graphic designer.

CURRENT JOB: Internet instructor.

TAKING CARE OF BUSINESS

Molly Roberts has always kept busy; she had her first part-time job when she was 11, working as a junior counselor at a day camp. She worked as the office manager in her mother's real estate business, too, which is where she first used computers. She used the computer to calculate loans and enter real estate listings, and she ended up spending plenty of time with the user manuals and online help.

Roberts studied English and political science in college and was thinking of going on to law school. But when she heard that most law students never become lawyers anyway—many go into research or become lobbyists—she changed her mind. Instead she took a job with a bank, as a graphic designer in their investment division. She had to use investment statistics to create charts and graphs for presentations; the job required strong computing experience, and Roberts was interested in investing, so it seemed a good fit.

A JOB WITH THE BANK

Roberts stayed with the bank for about 18 months and then worked for herself for about eight months doing Internet design—creating World Wide Web pages. But she found marketing herself and running the business at the same time difficult, so when she saw an ad from Prosoft looking for trainers, she jumped at the opportunity. Prosoft needed people-oriented people; the company could teach the technical skills, they said, but the most important thing was for the trainers to be comfortable working with people.

Roberts had a feeling that this was the perfect job for her. She's since discovered that she was right, and she's never been happier with a job than she is now. She travels a lot, all over the United States, from California to New York to Texas. She teaches people about HTML (HyperText Markup Language, the "coding" system used to create World Wide Web pages), multimedia, Web site creation software, and even about JavaScript (a scripting language used on many Web sites).

IT'S SHOWBIZ

Roberts feels that she's part entertainer. "If you don't like to talk in front of people, avoid this career," she says. "You have to be able to get up in front of room full of people and entertain them; training is part teaching and part showbiz." A good trainer doesn't just recite a list of facts. You have to make the training session—the "show"—interesting and lively.

"This can be a challenging job," Roberts says. "You often have people from a wide variety of backgrounds and computer experience in the same class, so you have to keep the experts happy while not losing the novices." This is especially true of the Internet, her specialty. Because it's so new, it's difficult to get a class full of people at the same technical level. "You need to be flexible, able to change the flow of the class at any moment. Whenever I start a lesson, I have seven different game plans I can follow, just in case."

Roberts expects to continue in training for now, though she'd like to branch out a little. She'd like to write courseware, the lesson plans that trainers work from, and might also enjoy writing training manuals, books used by individuals to train themselves. For the moment, however, she feels that she's in the right job at the right time.

Webmaster

SKILL SET

✔ ART

✔ COMPUTERS

✔ WRITING

WHAT IS A WEBMASTER?

A webmaster is . . . well, it depends on who you ask. Some people put together a basic one-page home page on the Internet and declare themselves webmasters. In fact, if you look at all the homemade pages credited to "webmasters," you might get the idea that this is the fastest-growing profession on the planet. It's a growing profession all right, but it's not quite as easy as it might look on the surface.

A webmaster is someone who creates Web sites on the World Wide Web. Webmasters apply a number of skills and resources to design, create, and maintain effective Web sites on behalf of their own companies, an employer, or any number of clients. The skills required vary widely. At a minimum, the webmaster must be able to create Web sites, so graphic design and writing skills are useful here. Webmasters may also be involved in promoting the Web site—that is, "getting the word out" so that people visit the site—requiring skills such as marketing and project management.

A few webmasters take over the role of Web-server administrator, as well; that is, they not only create the site but even keep the Web server running. For that, the ability to set up and maintain network connections is needed. It's no wonder that many of the larger and more complex sites are actually run by a team of professionals.

For the most part, webmasters wear three hats: information manager, HTML-page creator (a page creator in HyperText Markup Language), and graphic designer. As information manager, the webmaster is responsible for the thoughtful arrangement of large volumes of information. Think of this part of the process as if the webmaster were an information architect, having to arrange all the information in "rooms" and create a blueprint so that visitors can easily find their way to the information they need.

As HTML-page creator, the webmaster places the information into a form that can be displayed by a Web browser. HyperText Markup Language is the text-formatting language that all Web sites are written in. HTML uses simple codes to describe how each piece of text in a page should be displayed in a browser. It's relatively easy to learn—it's not like learning a programming language, which can be quite difficult—but there's quite a lot to it.

There are many programs that automatically create the pages. These are like word-processing programs for Web sites; you type the words, and the program enters the HTML codes for you. Nonetheless, most webmasters themselves understand quite a bit of HTML, as HTML programs are often limited to a relatively small set of HTML commands. To get really creative, a webmaster must understand how to go beyond the programs and enter some of the more advanced codes directly.

As graphic designer, the webmaster uses icons, graphics, color, and other elements of design to create an appealing look for the site. With millions of Web sites to choose from, competition keeps this phase of the process vital. The designer must create a unique identity that reflects the purpose of the site and the image that the client wishes to convey. With an ever-increasing amount of business being conducted on the Internet, the Web site is often the only contact a potential client has with a company, so it is especially important to make a good impression. Keeping the site fresh and exciting while maintaining a consistent look and feel are ongoing challenges for the webmaster.

Even though the career didn't even exist 10 years ago, opportunities for talented webmasters look promising for the future. There are no specific educational requirements for a webmaster, but the need for strong computer skills is obvious. Perhaps not so obvious is the need for equally strong communication skills. A degree in computer science can be a useful asset for a webmaster, but there's also room for the self-motivated, self-taught mavericks who continue to make an indelible mark on the computer profession.

 TRY IT OUT

WORLD WIDE WEB

Believe it or not, there was no such thing as the Internet when your parents were kids. Yours is the very first generation on earth to have access to a world of information at your fingertips. Use the following resources (and others you find on your own using, you got it, the World Wide Web) to create a timeline of the history of the Internet.

- ☼ A Brief History of the Internet at http://www.isoc. org/internet/history/brief.shtml
- ☼ How the Internet Works at http://computer. howstuffworks.com/internet-infrastructure.htm
- ☼ Internet on Wikipedia at http://en.wikipedia.org/ wiki/Internet
- ☼ Making Internet History at http://www.factmonster. com/spot/99internet1.html
- ☼ The World Wide Web: Origins and Beyond at http:// www.zeltser.com/web-history

MAKE A PLAN

Put on the webmaster's information manager hat, and gather all the information you can about your school. You might include the school directory, yearbook, newsletters, staff résumés, sports schedules, and calendar of special events. Use poster board to make a blueprint of what information you'd include and how you'd organize it so that visitors could find the good stuff quickly and easily.

# CHECK IT OUT

🖱 ON THE WEB

DO-IT-YOURSELF WEBMASTER

See if you've got the right stuff to be a webmaster someday by using these online resources to make your own Web site:

- ☼ Create Your Own Web Page at http://www. smplanet.com/webpage/webpage.html
- ☼ Make Your Own Web Page http://www.girlpower. gov/girlarea/sciencetech/web/index.htm
- ☼ Web Genies at http://www.girlpower.gov/girlarea/ sciencetech/web/index.htm
- ☼ Web Monkey at http://hotwired.lycos.com/ webmonkey/kids

THE GOOD, THE BAD, AND THE UGLY

Successful webmasters know the difference between good Web sites and bad ones. See if you can tell the difference by comparing good sites featured on http://www.kidsites.com and the worst ones featured on http://www.webpagesthatsuck.com.

In addition, find links to all kinds of interesting sites used by professional webmasters at http://www.cio.com/WebMaster/wm_notebook_front.htm.

AT THE LIBRARY

WEB BROWSING

Learn more about the Web, Web sites, and what it takes to be a webmaster in the following books:

Brown, Marty. *Cool Careers: Webmaster.* New York: Rosen, 2003.

Perry, Robert. *Build Your Own Website.* Danbury, Conn.: Franklin Watts, 2000.

Oleksy, Walter. *Web Page Designer.* New York: Rosen Publishing, 2000.

Spangenburg, Ray. *Savvy Surfing on the Internet: Searching and Evaluating Websites.* Berkeley Heights, N.J.: Enslow Publishers, 2001.

Stewart, Melissa. *Tim Berners-Lee: Inventor of the World Wide Web.* New York: Ferguson, 2001.

WITH THE EXPERTS

International Webmasters Association
119 East Union Street, Suite F
Pasadena, CA 91103
http://www.iwanet.org

World Organization of Webmasters
9850 Oak Avenue Parkway, Suite 7-177
Folsom, CA 95630
http://www.joinwow.org

GET ACQUAINTED

Jeni Li Shoecraft, Webmaster

CAREER PATH

CHILDHOOD ASPIRATION:
To be president of the United States and later to be a foreign language interpreter for the United Nations.

FIRST JOB: Data entry clerk in her dad's office.

CURRENT JOB: Senior systems programmer at Arizona State University.

WHAT'S ONE MORE LANGUAGE?

Jeni Li Shoecraft has always enjoyed learning new languages. She studied Latin, German, French, and Spanish in high school and college and is currently learning Japanese. All this has prepared her to think and communicate in new ways. When it came time to study computer programming languages, Shoecraft was ready and willing to add some new ones to her résumé.

FINDING A FUTURE

Along with discovering a natural affinity for languages there, high school was the place where Shoecraft fell in love with computers. This discovery actually came in a roundabout way. She'd taken a computer typing class, liked the teacher, and really liked one of the boys in the class. Given the option to take a computer programming class the next semester, she took it. By the end of the semester, the boy was history, but computers were her destiny.

About that same time, Shoecraft's father decided she needed a job and hired her to do data entry in his office. It was boring work, but when Shoecraft discovered a glitch in the system, she got the chance to write—for pay for the first time—a program to fix it. Now that's initiative!

ONE MINUTE SHE WAS DANCING . . .

While in college, one of Shoecraft's favorite ways to relax after a day in class was to attend dance jams—no drinking, no smoking, just lots of great dancing. One night she met someone, and they began talking about their mutual interest in computers. He set up an interview with his boss, and the next thing Shoecraft knew, she had a job in sales and technical support for a small computer firm. The position provided just the experience she needed to augment her computer science degree and help her land a position in the computer division of Arizona State University (ASU).

ON TO BIGGER AND BETTER THINGS

The ASU job involved providing computer support for faculty and staff at the West campus as well as installing software, training, and writing documentation for computer users. It was fun and interesting work. But, since her goal at any job is to work herself out of a position, she soon found many ways to help the staff help themselves, which left more time for other fun and interesting work. In her spare time she discovered the World Wide Web and loved it. So she taught herself enough HTML to create a personal Web site.

THE RIGHT PLACE AT THE RIGHT TIME

Perfect timing came into play at this point. Shoecraft was hooked on the Web and getting pretty good at finding her way around the system. At the same time, her department was asked to develop an interactive project for the university's internal Web, and Shoecraft's boss tapped her newfound skill for the task. The first project was a hit with the boss and with Shoecraft. On the project, she worked hard to develop a good relationship with the university Web staff, which made working together a breeze when she became campus webmaster.

Being close to the university Web staff also meant that Shoecraft was one of the first to know when a Web position became available 35 miles closer to home at a different ASU campus. The result of all her effort was that she worked herself right into a brand-new position as webmaster for the ASU Web site.

The moral of the story behind Shoecraft's interesting career progression is that you should keep learning and stay a step ahead of your current position. You just never know where this path will lead, but it tends to offer a beeline toward better opportunities.

MAKE A COMPUTER DETOUR!

Computers are entering every area of life and work. This book has given you an overview of a few ways in which computers are being used. But there are thousands more. The following list provides more ideas for making computers a focal point of your career. These ideas are grouped in categories to help you narrow down specific interest areas. Use them as a starting point to search out the best spot for your computer interests and abilities.

To make the most of this phase of your exploration, draw up a list of the ideas that you'd like to learn more about. Look them up in a career encyclopedia and get acquainted with more possibilities for your future!

When you come across a particularly intriguing occupation, use the form on pages 170–171 to record your discoveries.

A WORLD OF COMPUTER CAREERS

HARDWARE

These professions involve working with the "guts" of the computer, developing bigger and better technology that continues to revolutionize the workplace. Innovation, computer expertise, and logical thinking are common traits of all kinds of hardware professionals.

computer chip designer
computer chip manufacturing
  technician
computer designer

computer development engineer
electrical engineer
manufacturing engineer
semiconductor engineer

SOFTWARE

Software professionals do the thinking behind everything a computer does, from very simple commands to extremely complicated computerized tasks. Creativity, the ability to break complex tasks into minute steps, and effective communication skills are important assets for most types of software professionals.

CD-ROM producer
computer game animator
computer game programmer
database designer
entertainment software writer
freelance computer programmer
graphical user interface designer

quality assurance manager
software engineer
software integration engineer
software project manager
software tester
software tools developer
virtual reality developer

SERVICES FOR COMPUTER USERS

Computer service occupations tend to blend equal parts of computer expertise and communication skills. In various ways, they help users maximize the potential of their computer systems.

computer consultant
computer science teacher
computer service bureau manager

cyberlibrarian
data retrieval specialist
freelance technical writer

INFORMATION SYSTEMS MANAGEMENT

Working with lots of information and lots of computer power summarizes what's involved in information systems management. These professionals must have exceptional computer skills as well as the ability to manage other people, information, and technology.

database administrator
manager of information
   systems (MIS)

network manager
systems administrator
systems integrator

NETWORK AND ONLINE SERVICES

The opportunities in this arena continue to grow. The more uses people find for the Internet, the more work there will be to keep things running smoothly.

Internet access provider
Internet promotions consultant
Internet service provider
   systems administrator
Internet storefront operator

intranet specialist
local area network (LAN)
   specialist
systems operator (SYSOP
Web server administrator

SALES AND INFORMATION SERVICES

These options provide ways to blend an interest in computers with other types of talent. Whether it's a gift for gab or a way with the written word, there's a way to put it to work here.

computer book author
computer book editor
computer consultant recruiter
computer industry reporter
computer magazine writer

computer sales representative
computer store owner
public relations manager
software industry analyst
trade show promoter

COMPUTER-RELIANT JOBS—
SPECIALIZED AND NONSPECIALIZED

The possibilities here are endless. Virtually any type of business or industry has been touched in one way or another by computers. See how many other ideas you can add to this list.

aircraft designer
artist
automobile designer
cable network digital system
 analyst
cartoonist
computer-aided design (CAD)
 illustrator
computer-aided design (CAD)
 manager
computer-aided manufacture
 (CAM) engineer
computer animator
computer musician
consumer product research

data entry clerk
desktop publisher
electronic publisher
graphic designer
musical instrument digital
 interface (MIDI) engineer
newsletter publisher
printing typesetter
receptionist
reservations clerk
secretary
virtual reality entertainment
 center operator
word processor operator
zine publisher

DON'T STOP NOW!

GO FOR IT!

It's been a fast-paced trip so far. Take a break, regroup, and look at all the progress you've made.

1st Stop: Discover
You discovered some personal interests and natural abilities that you can start building a career around.

2nd Stop: Explore
You've explored an exciting array of career opportunities in this field. You're now aware that your career can involve either a specialized area with many educational requirements or that it can involve a practical application of computer science methods with a minimum of training and experience.

At this point, you've found a couple careers that make you wonder "Is this a good option for me?" Now it's time to put it all together and make an informed, intelligent choice. It's time to get a sense of what it might be like to have a job like the one(s) you're considering. In other words, it's time to move on to step three and do a little experimenting with success.

3rd Stop: Experiment

By the time you finish this section, you'll have reached one of three points in the career planning process.

1. **Green light!** You found it. No need to look any further. This is the career for you. (This may happen to a lucky few. Don't worry if it hasn't happened yet for you. This whole process is about exploring options, experimenting with ideas, and, eventually, making the best choice for you.)

2. **Yellow light!** Close but not quite. You seem to be on the right path, but you haven't nailed things down for sure. (This is where many people your age end up, and it's a good place to be. You've learned what it takes to really check things out. Hang in there. Your time will come.)

3. **Red light!** Whoa! No doubt about it, this career just isn't for you. (Congratulations! Aren't you glad you found out now and not after you'd spent four years in college preparing for this career? Your next stop: Make a U-turn and start this process over with another career.)

Here's a sneak peek at what you'll be doing in the next section.

- First you'll pick a favorite career idea (or two or three).
- Second, you'll link up with a whole world of great information about that career on the Internet (it's easier than you think).
- Third, you'll snoop around the library to find answers to the top 10 things you've just got to know about your future career.
- Fourth, you'll either write a letter or use the Internet to request information from a professional organization associated with this career.
- Fifth, you'll chat on the phone to conduct a telephone interview.

After all that you'll (finally!) be ready to put it all together in your very own Career Ideas for Kids career profile (see page 170).

Hang on to your hats and get ready to make tracks!

#1 NARROW DOWN YOUR CHOICES

You've been introduced to quite a few computer career ideas. You may also have some ideas of your own to add. Which ones appeal to you the most?

Write your top three choices in the spaces below. (Sorry if this is starting to sound like a broken record, but . . . if this book does not belong to you, write your responses on a separate sheet of paper.)

1. _____

2. _____

3. _____

#2 SURF THE NET

With the Internet, you have a world of information at your fingertips. The Internet has something for everyone, and it's getting easier to access all the time. An increasing number of libraries and schools are offering access to the Internet on their computers, or you may have a computer at home.

A typical career search will land everything from the latest news on developments in the field and course notes from universities to museum exhibits, interactive games, educational activities, and more. You just can't beat the timeliness or the variety of information available on the Web.

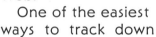

One of the easiest ways to track down this information is to use an Internet search engine, such as Yahoo! Simply type the topic you are looking for, and in a matter of seconds you'll have a list of options from around the world. For instance, if you are looking for information about companies that make candy, use the words "candy manufacturer" to start your search. It's fun to browse—you never know what you'll come up with.

Before you link up, keep in mind that many of these sites are geared toward professionals who are already working in a particular field. Some of the sites can get pretty technical. Just use the experience as a chance to nose around the field, hang out with the people who are tops in the field, and think about whether or not you'd like to be involved in a profession like that.

Specific sites to look for are the following:

Professional associations. Find out about what's happening in the field, conferences, journals, and other helpful tidbits.

Schools that specialize in this area. Many include research tools, introductory courses, and all kinds of interesting information.

Government agencies. Quite a few are going high-tech with lots of helpful resources.

Web sites hosted by experts in the field (this seems to be a popular hobby among many professionals). These Web sites are often as entertaining as they are informative.

   If you're not sure where to go, just start clicking around. Sites often link to other sites. You may want to jot down notes about favorite sites. Sometimes you can even print information that isn't copyright-protected; try the print option and see what happens.
   Be prepared: Surfing the Internet can be an addicting habit! There is so much awesome information. It's a fun way to focus on your future.
   Write the addresses of the three best Web sites that you find during your search in the space below (or on a separate sheet of paper if this book does not belong to you).

1. _____

2. _____

3. _____

#3 SNOOP AT THE LIBRARY

Take your list of favor-
ite career ideas, a
notebook, and a help-
ful adult with you to
the library. When you
get there, go to the
reference section and
ask the librarian to help
you find books about
careers. Most libraries
will have at least one set

of career encyclopedias. Some of the larger libraries may also have career information on CD-ROM.

Gather all the information you can and use it to answer the following questions in your notebook about each of the careers on your list. Make sure to ask for help if you get stuck.

TOP 10 THINGS YOU NEED TO KNOW ABOUT YOUR CAREER

1. What is the purpose of this job?

   _____

2. What kind of place is this type of work usually done in? For example, would I work mostly in a busy office, outdoors, or in a laboratory?

   _____

3. What kind of time is required to do this job? For instance, is the job usually performed during regular daytime business hours or do people work various shifts around the clock?

   _____

4. What kinds of tools are used to do this job?

   _____

5. In what ways does this job involve working with other people?

   _____

6. What kind of preparation does a person need to qualify for this job?

   _____

7. What kinds of skills and abilities are needed to be successful in this type of work?

_____

8. What's a typical day on the job like?

_____

_____

9. How much money can I expect to earn as a beginner?

_____

10. What kind of classes do I need to take in high school to get ready for this type of work?

_____

#4 GET IN TOUCH WITH THE EXPERTS

One of the best places to find information about a particular career is a professional organization devoted especially to that career. After all, these organizations are full of the best and the brightest professionals working in that particular field. Who could possibly know more about how the work gets done? There are more than 450,000 organizations in the United States, so there is bound to be an association related to just about any career you can possibly imagine.

There are a couple ways you can find these organizations:

1. Look at the "Check It Out—With the Experts" list following a career you found especially interesting in the Take A Trip! section of this book.

2. Go online and use your favorite search engine (such as http://www.google.com or http://yahoo.com) to find professional associations related to a career you are

interested in. You might use the name of the career, plus the words "professional association" to start your search. You're likely to find lots of useful information online, so keep looking until you hit pay dirt.

3. Go to the reference section of your public library and ask the librarian to help you find a specific type of association in a reference book called *Encyclopedia of Associations* (Farmington Hills, Mich.: Thomson Gale) Or, if your library has access to it, the librarian may suggest using an online database called *Associations Unlimited* (Farmington Hills, Mich.: Thomson Gale).

Once you've tracked down a likely source of information, there are two ways to get in touch with a professional organization.

1. Send an e-mail.
   Most organizations include a "contact us" button on their Web sites. Sometimes this e-mail is directed to a webmaster or a customer service representative. An e-mail request might look something like this:

   Subject: Request for Information
   Date: 2/1/2008 3:18:41 PM Eastern Standard Time
   From: janedoe@mycomputer.com
   To: webmaster@candyloversassociation.org

   I am a fifth grade student, and I am interested in learning more about careers for candy lovers. Would you please send me any information you have about what people do in your industry?

   Thank you very much.
   Jane Doe

2. Write a letter requesting information.
   Your letter should be either typed on a computer or written in your best handwriting. It should include the date, the complete address of the organization you are contacting, a salutation or greeting, a brief

description of your request, and a signature. Make sure to include an address where the organization can reach you with a reply. Something like the following letter would work just fine.

Dear Sir or Madam:

I am a fifth grade student, and I would like to learn more about what it is like to work in the candy lover profession. Would you please send me information about careers? My address is 456 Main Street, Anytown, USA 54321.

Thank you very much.

Sincerely,
Jane Doe

Write the names and addresses of the professional organizations you discover on a separate sheet of paper.

#5 CHAT ON THE PHONE

Talking to a seasoned professional—someone who experiences the job day in and day out—can be a great way to get the inside story on what a career is all about. Fortunately for you, the experts in any career field can be as close as the nearest telephone.

Sure, it can be a bit scary calling up an adult whom you don't know. But two things are in your favor:

1. They can't see you. The worst thing they can do is hang up on you, so just relax and enjoy the conversation.

2. They'll probably be happy to talk to you about their job. In fact, most people will be flattered that you've called. If you happen to contact someone who seems reluctant to talk, thank them for their time and try someone else.

Here are a few pointers to help make your telephone interview a success:

☼ Mind your manners and speak clearly.
☼ Be respectful of their time and position.
☼ Be prepared with good questions and
   take notes as you talk.

One more common sense reminder: be careful about giving out your address and DO NOT arrange to meet anyone you don't know without your parents' supervision.

TRACKING DOWN CAREER EXPERTS

You might be wondering by now how to find someone to interview. Have no fear! It's easy if you're persistent. All you have to do is ask. Ask the right people and you'll have a great lead in no time.

A few of the people to ask and sources to turn to are:

Your parents. They may know someone (or know someone who knows someone) who has just the kind of job you're looking for.

Your friends and neighbors. You might be surprised to find out how many interesting jobs these people have when you start asking them what they (or their parents) do for a living.

Librarians. Since you've already figured out what kinds of companies employ people in your field of interest, the next step is to ask for information about local employers. Although it's a bit cumbersome to use, a big volume called *Contacts Influential* can provide this kind of information.

Professional associations. Call, e-mail, or write to the professional associations you discovered using the activity on pages 163–165 and ask for recommendations.

Chambers of commerce. The local chamber of commerce probably has a directory of employers, their specialties, and their phone numbers. Call the chamber, explain what you are looking for, and give them a chance to help their future workforce.

Newspaper and magazine articles. Find an article about the subject you are interested in. Chances are pretty good that it will mention the name of at least one expert in the field. The article probably won't include the person's phone number (that would be too easy), so you'll have to look for clues. Common clues include the name of the company that they work for, the town that they live in, and if the person is an author, the name of their publisher. Make a few phone calls and track them down (if long distance calls are involved, make sure to get your parents' permission first).

INQUIRING KIDS WANT TO KNOW

Before you make the call, make a list of questions to ask. You'll cover more ground if you focus on using the five W's (and the H) that you've probably heard about in your creative writing classes: Who? What? Where? When? How? and Why? For example:

1. Whom do you work for?

   _____

2. What is a typical workday like for you?

   _____

3. Where can I get some on-the-job experience?

   _____

4. When did you become a _____?
   (profession)

5. How much can you earn in this profession? (But remember it's not polite to ask someone how much *he* or *she* earns.)

_____

6. Why did you choose this profession?

_____

Use a grid like the one below to keep track of the questions you ask in the boxes labeled "Q" and the answers you receive in the boxes labeled "A."

Who?	What?	Where?	When?	How?	Why?
Q	Q	Q	Q	Q	Q
A	A	A	A	A	A
Q	Q	Q	Q	Q	Q
A	A	A	A	A	A

One last suggestion: Add a professional (and very classy) touch to the interview process by following up with a thank-you note to the person who took time out of a busy schedule to talk with you.

#6 INFORMATION IS POWER

As you may have noticed, a similar pattern of information was used for each of the careers profiled in this book. Each entry included:

- ⚲ a general description of the career
- ⚲ Try It Out activities to give readers a chance to find out what's its really like to do each job
- ⚲ a list of Web sites, library resources, and professional organizations to check for more information
- ⚲ a get-acquainted interview with a professional

You may have also noticed that all the information you just gathered would fit rather nicely in a Career Ideas for Kids career profile of your own. Just fill in the blanks on the following pages to get your thoughts together (or, if this book does not belong to you, use a separate sheet of paper).

And by the way, this formula is one that you can use throughout your life to help you make fully informed career choices.

CAREER TITLE _____

WHAT IS A _____ ?

Use career encyclopedias and other resources to write a description of this
career.

_____

_____

_____

_____

SKILL SET

✔ _____

✔ _____

✔ _____

☞ TRY IT OUT

Write project ideas here. Ask your parents and your teacher
to come up with a plan.

_____

_____

_____

_____

_____

✔ CHECK IT OUT

🖱 ON THE WEB

List Internet addresses of interesting Web sites you find.

_____

_____

_____

_____

_____

📚 AT THE LIBRARY

List the titles and authors of books about this career.

_____

_____

_____

_____

_____

🗣 WITH THE EXPERTS

List professional organizations where you can learn more about this profession.

_____

_____

_____

_____

_____

GET ACQUAINTED

Interview a professional in the field and summarize your findings.

_____

_____

_____

_____

_____

_____

_____

_____

WHAT'S NEXT?

Whoa, everybody! At this point, you've put in some serious miles on your career exploration journey. Before you move on, let's put things in reverse for just a sec and take another look at some of the clues you uncovered about yourself when you completed the "discover" activities in the Get in Gear chapter on pages 7 to 26.

The following activities will help lay the clues you learned about yourself alongside the clues you learned about a favorite career idea. The comparison will help you decide if that particular career idea is a good idea for you to pursue. It doesn't matter if a certain career sounds absolutely amazing. If it doesn't honor your skills, your interests, and your values, it's not going to work for you.

The first time you looked at these activities, they were numbered one through five as "Discover" activities. This time around they are numbered in the same order but labeled "Rediscover" activities. That's not done to confuse you (sure hope it doesn't!). Instead, it's done to drive home a very important point that this is an important process you'll want to revisit time and time again as you venture throughout your career—now and later.

First, pick the one career idea that you are most interested in at this point and write its name here (or if this book doesn't belong to you, blah, blah, blah—you know the drill by now):

_____

With that idea in mind, revisit your responses to the following Get in Gear activities and complete the following:

REDISCOVER #1: WATCH FOR SIGNS ALONG THE WAY

Based on your responses to the statements on page 8, choose which of the following road signs best describes how you feel about your career idea:

- ♀ Green light—Go! Go! Go! This career idea is a perfect fit!
- ♀ Yellow light—Proceed with caution! This career idea is a good possibility, but you're not quite sure that it's the "one" just yet.
- ♀ Stop—Hit the brakes! There's no doubt about it—this career idea is definitely not for you!

REDISCOVER #2: RULES OF THE ROAD

Take another look at the work-values chart you made on page 16. Now use the same symbols to create a work-values chart for the career idea you are considering. After you have all the symbols in place, compare the two charts and answer these questions:

- ☼ Does your career idea's **purpose** line up with yours? Would it allow you to work in the kinds of **place** you most want to work in?
- ☼ What about the **time** commitment—is it in sync with what you're hoping for?
- ☼ Does it let you work with the **tools** and the kind of **people** you most want to work with?
- ☼ And, last but not least, are you willing to do what it takes to **prepare** for a career like this?

PURPOSE	PLACE	TIME
TOOLS	PEOPLE	PREPARATION

REDISCOVER #3: DANGEROUS DETOURS

Go back to page 16 and double-check your list of 10 careers that you hope to avoid at any cost.
Is this career on that list? ____Yes _____ No
Should it be? ____Yes _____ No

REDISCOVER #4:
ULTIMATE CAREER DESTINATION

Pull out the ultimate career destination brochure you made (as described on page 17). Use a pencil to cross through every reference to "my ideal career" and replace it with the name of the career idea you are now considering.

Is the brochure still true? _____Yes _____ No

If not, what would you change on the brochure to make it true?

REDISCOVER #5:
GET SOME DIRECTION

Quick! Think fast! What is your personal Skill Set as discovered on page 26?

Write down your top three interest areas:

1. _____

2. _____

3. _____

What three interest areas are most closely associated with your career idea?

1. _____

2. _____

3. _____

Does this career's interest areas match any of yours?
_____Yes _____ No

Now the big question: Are you headed in the right direction?

If so, here are some suggestions to keep you moving ahead:

- ☼ Keep learning all you can about this career—read, surf the Web, talk to people, and so on. In other words, keep using some of the strategies you used in the Don't Stop Now chapter on pages 157 to 171 to do all you can to make a fully informed career decision.
- ☼ Work hard in school and get good grades. What you do now counts! Your performance, your behavior, your attitude—all conspire to either propel you forward or hold you back.
- ☼ Get involved in clubs and other after-school activities to further develop your interests and skills. Whether it's student government, 4-H, or sports, these kinds of activities give you a chance to try new things and gain confidence in your abilities.

If not, here are some suggestions to help you regroup:

- ☼ Read other books in the Career Ideas for Kids series to explore options associated with you other interest areas.
- ☼ Take a variety of classes in school and get involved in different kids of after-school activities to get a better sense of what you like and what you do well.
- ☼ Talk to your school guidance counselor about taking a career assessment test to help fine tune your focus.
- ☼ Most of all, remember that time is on your side. Use the next few years to discover more about yourself, explore the options, and experiment with what it will take to make you succeed. Keep at it and look forward to a fantastic future!

HOORAY! YOU DID IT!

This has been quite a trip. If someone tries to tell you that this process is easy, don't believe them. Figuring out what you want to do with the rest of your life is heavy stuff, and it should be. If you don't put some thought (and some sweat and hard work) into the process, you'll get stuck with whatever comes your way.

You may not have things planned to a T. Actually, it's probably better if you don't. You'll change some of your ideas as you grow and experience new things. And, you may find an interesting detour or two along the way. That's OK.

The most important thing about beginning this process now is that you've started to dream. You've discovered that you have some unique talents and abilities to share. You've become aware of some of the ways you can use them to make a living—and perhaps make a difference in the world.

Whatever you do, don't lose sight of the hopes and dreams you've discovered. You've got your entire future ahead of you. Use it wisely.

PASSPORT TO YOUR FUTURE

Getting where you want to go requires patience, focus, and lots of hard work. It also hinges on making good choices. Following is a list of some surefire ways to give yourself the best shot at a bright future. Are you up to the challenge? Can you do it? Do you dare?

Put your initials next to each item that you absolutely promise to do.

___ ☿ Do my best in every class at school
___ ☿ Take advantage of every opportunity to get a wide variety of experiences through participation in sports, after-school activities, at my favorite place of worship, and in my community
___ ☿ Ask my parents, teachers, or other trusted adults for help when I need it
___ ☿ Stay away from drugs, alcohol, and other bad scenes that can rob me of a future before I even get there
___ ☿ Graduate from high school

SOME FUTURE DESTINATIONS

Wow! Look how far you've come! By now you should be well-equipped to discover, explore, and experiment your way to an absolutely fantastic future. To keep you headed in the right direction, this section will point you toward useful resources that provide more insight, information, and inspiration as you continue your quest to find the perfect career.

IT'S NOT JUST FOR NERDS

The school counselor's office is not just a place where teachers send troublemakers. One of its main purposes is to help students like you make the most of your educational opportunities. Most schools will have a number of useful resources, including career assessment tools (ask about the Self-Directed Search Career Explorer or the COPS Interest

Inventory—these are especially useful assessments for people your age). They may also have a stash of books, videos, and other helpful materials.

Make sure no one's looking and sneak into your school counseling office to get some expert advice!

AWESOME INTERNET CAREER RESOURCES

Your parents will be green with envy when they see all the career planning resources you have at your fingertips. Get ready to hear them whine, "But they didn't have all this stuff when I was a kid." Make the most of these cyberspace opportunities.

☀ **Adventures in Education**
http://adventuresineducation.org/middleschool
Here you'll find some useful tools to make the most of your education—starting now. Make sure to watch "The Great College Mystery," an online animation featuring Dr. Ed.

☀ **America's Career Info Net**
http://www.acinet.org
Career sites don't get any bigger than this one! Compliments of the U.S. Department of Labor, and a chunk of your parent's tax dollars, you'll find all kinds of information about what people do, how much money they make, and where they work. Although it's mostly geared toward adults, you may want to take a look at some of the videos (the site has links to more than 450!) that show people at work.

☀ **ASVAB Career Exploration Program**
http://www.asvabprogram.com
This site may prove especially useful as you continue to think through various options. It includes sections

for students to learn about themselves, to explore careers, and to plan for their futures.

☼ Career Voyages
http://www.careervoyages.gov
This site will be especially helpful to you as you get a little older. It offers four paths to get you started: "Where do I start?" "Which industries are growing?" "How do I qualify and get a job?" and "Does education pay? How do I pay?" However, it also includes a special section especially for elementary school students. Just click the button that says "Still in elementary school?" or go to http://www.careervoyages. gov/students-elementary.cfm.

☼ Job Profiles
http://jobprofiles.org
This site presents the personal side of work with profiles of people working in jobs associated with agriculture and nature, arts and sports, business and communications, construction and manufacturing, education and science, government, health and social services, retail and wholesale, and other industries.

☼ Major and Careers Central
http://www.collegeboard.com/csearch/majors_careers
This site is hosted by the College Board (the organization responsible for a very important test called the SAT, which you're likely to encounter if you plan to go to college). It includes helpful information about how different kinds of subjects you can study in college can prepare you for specific types of jobs.

☼ Mapping Your Future
http://mapping-your-future.org/MHSS/

This site provides strategies and resources for students as they progress through middle school and high school.

☼ My Cool Career

http://www.mycoolcareer.com
This site is where you can take free online self-assessment quizzes, explore your dreams, and listen to people with interesting jobs talk about their work.

☼ O*NET Online

http://online.onetcenter.org
This U.S. Department of Labor site provides comprehensive information about hundreds of important occupations. Although you may need to ask a parent or teacher to help you figure out how to use the system, it can be a good source of digging for nitty-gritty details about a specific type of job. For instance, each profile includes a description of the skills, abilities, and special knowledge needed to perform each job.

☼ Think College Early

http://www.ed.gov/students/prep/college/
thinkcollege/early/edlite-tcehome.html
Even though you almost need a college degree just to type the Web address for this U.S. Department of Education site, it contains some really cool career information and helps you think about how college might fit into your future plans.

☼ What Interests You?

http://www.bls.gov/k12
This Bureau of Labor Statistics site is geared toward students. It lets you explore careers by interests such as reading, building and fixing things, managing money, helping people, and more.

JOIN THE CLUB

Once you've completed eighth grade, you are eligible to check out local opportunities to participate in Learning for Life's career education programs. Some communities offer Explorer posts that sponsor activities with students interested in industries that include the arts and humanities, aviation, business, communications, engineering, fire service, health, law enforcement, law and government, science, skilled trades, or social services. To find a local office, go to http://www.learning-for-life.org/exploring/main.html and type your zip code.

Until then, you can go online and play *Life Choices*, a really fun and challenging game where you get one of five virtual jobs at http://www.learning-for-life.org/games/LCSH/index.html.

MORE CAREER BOOKS ESPECIALLY FOR KIDS

It's especially important that people your age find out all they can about as many different careers as they can. Books like the ones listed below can introduce all kinds of interesting ideas that you might not encounter in your everyday life.

Greenfeld, Barbara C., and Robert A. Weinstein. *The Kids' College Almanac: A First Look at College.* Indianapolis, Ind.: JIST Works, 2001.
Young Person's Occupational Outlook Handbook. Indianapolis, Ind.: JIST Works, 2005.

Following are brief descriptions of several series of books geared especially toward kids like you. To find copies of these books, ask your school or public librarian to help you search the card file or library computer system using the name of the series.

Career Connections (published by UXL)
This extensive series features information and illustrations about jobs of interest to people interested in art and design, entrepreneurship, food, government and law, history, math and computers, and the performing arts as well as those who want to work with their hands or with living things.

Career Ideas for Kids (written by Diane Lindsey Reeves, published by Ferguson)
This series of interactive career exploration books features 10 different titles for kids who like adventure and travel, animals and nature, art, computers, math and money, music and dance, science, sports, talking, and writing.

Careers Without College (published by Peterson's)
These books offer a look at options available to those who prefer to find jobs that do not require a college degree and include titles focusing on cars, computers, fashion, fitness, healthcare, and music.

Cool Careers (published by Rosen Publishing)
Each title in this series focuses on a cutting-edge occupation such as computer animator, hardware engineer, multimedia and new media developer, video game designer, Web entrepreneur, and webmaster.

Discovering Careers for Your Future (published by Ferguson)
This series includes a wide range of titles that include those that focus on adventure, art, construction, fashion, film, history, nature, publishing, and radio and television.

Risky Business (written by Keith Elliot Greenberg, published by Blackbirch Press)
These books feature stories about people with adventurous types of jobs and include titles about a bomb squad officer, disease detective, marine biologist, photojournalist, rodeo clown, smoke jumper, storm chaser, stunt woman, test pilot, and wildlife special agent.

HEAVY-DUTY RESOURCES

Career encyclopedias provide general information about a lot of professions and can be a great place to start a career search. Those listed here are easy to use and provide useful information about nearly a zillion different jobs. Look for them in the reference section of your local library.

Career Discovery Encyclopedia, 6th ed. New York: Ferguson, 2006.

Careers for the 21st Century. Farmington Hills, Mich.: Lucent Books, 2002.

Children's Dictionary of Occupations. Princeton, N.J.: Cambridge Educational, 2004.

Encyclopedia of Career and Vocational Guidance. New York: Ferguson, 2005.

Farr, Michael, and Laurence Shatkin. *Enhanced Occupational Outlook Handbook.* 6th ed. Indianapolis, Ind.: JIST Works, 2006.

Occupational Outlook Handbook. Washington, D.C.: U.S. Government Printing Office, 2006.

FINDING PLACES TO WORK

Even though you probably aren't quite yet in the market for a real job, you can learn a lot about the kinds of jobs you might find if you were looking by visiting some of the most popular job-hunting sites on the Internet. Two particularly good ones to investigate are America's Job Bank (http://www.ajb. org) and Monster (http://www. monster.com).

INDEX

Page numbers in **boldface** indicate main articles. Page numbers in *italics* indicate photographs.

A

AbuGhazaleh, Elias 125–27, *125*
activities, appealing 18–23
AI *See* artificial intelligence scientist
AI Magazine 29
America's Job Bank 187
artificial intelligence scientist **29–38**
associations, professional computer
    finding and contacting 160, 163–68
    for artificial intelligence 35
    for computer operations 109, 116
    for game designers 44
    for hardware engineers 59, 60
    for Internet systems administrators 69
    for multimedia development 77–78
    for online research 85, 87
    for programming 53
    for repair technicians 92
    for shareware 100
    for software 100
    for technical support representatives 124
    for technical writing 132–33
    for trainers 141
    for webmasters 148

B

Babbage, Charles 49
biomimetics 72

books
on all careers 185–87
on artificial intelligence 34–35
on codes 68
on colleges 185
on communication skills 123–24, 140–41
on computer careers 161–63
on computer contacts 166
on computer game design 43–44
on computer programming 52–53
on computers 108, 112
on entrepreneurs 99–100
on hardware engineers 59–60
on the Internet and Internet administration 68
on multimedia development 77, 80
on mysteries 108
on online research 84–85
on programming 44
on repair technicians 88, 92
on science experiments 58
on software entrepreneurs 95
on speaking 140
on technology 116
on Web site design 148
on writing 128, 132

C
career profile, form for 170–71
careers to avoid, form for 16–17
cellular field operations manager 118
chamber of commerce 167
chat, computer 33
chief technology officer (CTO) 113
choices
making good 180
narrowing down your computer career 159
codes, cracking 68
computer-reliant jobs 156
computer service occupations 154–55
cookies, computer 29–30, 32
counseling, career 181–82
cracker, computer 66, 71
Curry, Brenda Dickson 133–35, 133

D
databases 54, 55, 97–98
database searching 81–82
detours, dangerous career 16–17
"Discover" activities **7–26**
diseases, computer diagnosis of 30–31
Drummond, Rachel 69–72, 69
DynaVox Technologies 101

E

experts, contacting
computer 163–68

F

family tree, researching your
83
forecasting, in business 62
freelancing 135, 136

G

game club, computer 42–
43
game designer, computer
39–47
games, online 42–43
See also specific online
games
government agencies,
finding on the Internet 161

H

hardware, careers in
computer **56–63**, 154
Hawkinson, Lowell 36–38,
36
help desk techs **119–27**
HyperText Markup Language
(HTML) 145–46

I

"I Have a Dream" speech
138–39
Iknowthat.com 100, 101–3

info-glut 37
information services 155
information systems
management 155
Internet, computer career
surfing on the 159–61
Internet service provider
(ISP) 64, 66
Internet systems
administrator **64–72**
interviews, with computer
experts 165–68

K

Kassel, Amelia 85–87, 85
Kidder, Tracy 60
Kiliany, Gary 100–103, 100
King, Martin Luther 138–39
Kolstad, Rob 109–11, 109
Kushdilian, Victor 53–55, 53

L

languages, computer
programming 34, 48–49
Learning for Life 185
Life Choices (online game)
185
Little, Mike 93–94, 93
Logo 34, 40, 41–42, 50
Lovelace, Ada 49

M

magazine articles, on
computer experts 167
mainframes 104–5

management information systems (MIS) director 113–14

math 41

models, modeling 31, 45

Monster 187

Moore, Gordon 50

multimedia developer **73–80**

N

Nabisco 29–30

nanotechnology 58–59

Net *See* Internet

network, computer 66–67

network services 155

newspaper articles, on computer experts 167

NovaStor Corporation 125–26

O

online researcher **81–87**

online services 155

P

PC Artificial Intelligence 29

Pemberton, John 61–63

people, in values clarification 9, 14, 16, 175

place, in values clarification 9, 11, 16, 175

planning, in business 62

PowerPoint 138

preparation, in values clarification 9, 15, 16, 175

problem solving 107

productivity, in business 62

programmer, computer **48–55**

programming, computer 34, 40, 44, 48–55, 103

purpose, in values clarification 9, 10, 16, 175

puzzles, cyber 107

R

"Rediscover" activities 174–77

repair technician **88–94**

Roberts, Molly 141–43, *141*

robots 29, 33, 35

Roche, Art 78–80, *78*

S

sales, computer 155

shareware 97, 98

Shoecraft, Jeni Li 149–51, *149*

SimCity (online game) 29, 31, 46

Skill Set

required for specific jobs 29, 39, 48, 56, 64, 73, 81, 88, 95, 104, 112, 119, 128, 136, 144

your personal 26

software, careers in computer **95–103**, 154

source code 48

spammers 71

Sportsware 53, 54–55

storyboarding 41

storytelling, sensory 76

surfing, safe Internet 67
systems analyst **104–11**
systems manager **112–18**

T

teacher *See* trainer
technical service agencies
  134
technical support
  representative **119–27**
technical writer **128–35**
telephone, interviewing
  computer experts by 165–
  68
time, in values clarification
  9, 12, 16, 175
tools, in values clarification
  9, 13, 16, 175
trainer **136–43**
troubleshooting, in business
  62
tutor, computer 122

U

Unix 71
USA Computer Olympiad
  (USACO) 111

V

values clarification exercise
  7–26, 174–77
Vann, Timothy 117–18, *117*
vocabulary, building 131–32,
  140
voltmeter 90

W

webmaster **144–51**
Web site(s) 28
  artificial intelligence 33–
    34
  career exploration 182–
    84
  computer games 42–43
  computer history 50–51
  computer manufacturers
    115
  computer operations 119
  computer programming
    51–52
  computer puzzles 107
  creating **144–51**
  entrepreneurs 98–99
  hardware engineers 59
  help desks 122–23
  hosted by experts in
    their field 161
  the Internet and Internet
    administration 67, 146–
    47
  job-hunting 187
  Learning for Life 185
  multimedia development
    76–77
  nanotechnology 59
  news 139
  online tutorials 123
  professional associations
    163–64
  repair technicians 91–92
  search engines 83, 84
  shareware 98
  software entrepreneurs
    95

speeches 136
technology and tech
  support 115–16, 122–23
vocabulary 131–32, 140
Web page design 146–
  48

Web sites for kids 144
  writing 131
words, learning new 131–32,
  140
Wright, Will 45–47, 95
writing, technical **128–35**